Thura's Diary

A young girl's life in war-torn Baghdad

Thura Al-Windawi

Translated by Robin Bray

PUFFIN

PUFFIN BOOKS

Published by the Penguin Group
Penguin Books Ltd, 80 Strand, London WC2R 0RL, England
Penguin Group (USA), Inc., 375 Hudson Street, New York, New York 10014, USA
Penguin Books Australia Ltd, 250 Camberwell Road, Camberwell, Victoria 3124, Australia
Penguin Books Canada Ltd, 10 Alcorn Avenue, Toronto, Ontario, Canada M4V 3B2
Penguin Books India (P) Ltd, 11 Community Centre, Panchsheel Park, New Delhi – 110 017, India
Penguin Books (NZ) Ltd, Cnr Rosedale and Airborne Roads, Albany, Auckland, New Zealand
Penguin Books (South Africa) (Pty) Ltd, 24 Sturdee Avenue, Rosebank 2196, South Africa

Penguin Books Ltd, Registered Offices: 80 Strand, London WC2R 0RL, England

www.penguin.com

First published 2004
1

Set in Linotype Sabon
Typeset by Rowland Phototypesetting Ltd, Bury St Edmunds, Suffolk

Made and printed in England by Clays Ltd, St Ives plc

British Library Cataloguing in Publication Data
A CIP catalogue record for this book is available from the British Library

ISBN 0–141–31769–8

I dedicate this diary to the people of Iraq, America and Britain – and to people everywhere, who have lost loved-ones in war.

Thura

Acknowledgements

First, I must thank Janine di Giovanni, the British correspondent for *The Times*, who I got to know in Baghdad in March of last year, a few days before the war on Iraq started. She encouraged me to continue writing my diary and helped me to get it published.

I would also like to express my gratitude to the BBC correspondents who gave me so much encouragement after filming aspects of my life both before and after the war. I would especially like to mention correspondents Adam Brookes and Paul Wood, and their producer, Kate Peters.

Many thanks, also, to the team of journalists from American network television, who I worked with for eight days while fighting was still going on in parts of Iraq. By watching them, I learned to never give up on my dreams.

I am also grateful to Penguin for taking up my diary, especially Clare Hulton, who, all the way from London, kept an eye on my work in Baghdad.

I would like to give special thanks to Lee

Stetson, the dean of admissions at the University of Pennsylvania, who offered me a place in the 2003 freshman class and secured full financial-aid grants to fund my college education. Dean Stetson was extremely supportive from the day he heard of my story. He and his staff have continued that support since I have been in Philadelphia and their belief in me has changed my life.

The help that my father has given me has been truly unlimited. Ever since I was a little girl in primary school, he has always encouraged me to keep a diary, and it was he who gave me the confidence to keep writing even when I was surrounded by the nightmare of war. I offer him my gratitude and love.

Introduction

The war against Iraq began on 20 March 2003. Less than two months later, Saddam Hussein, the country's dictator for more than twenty years, was deposed, Baghdad had fallen and hundreds had died in the process. The actual war may have been short, but for the Iraqi people it was a terrifying ordeal and many lives have been changed forever.

Thura Al-Windawi started writing her diary a matter of days before the bombs started to fall on Baghdad. Then nineteen years old, she wrote as a way of controlling the chaos around her; as a way of staying calm and also in the hope that one day other people might understand what it was like for ordinary Iraqis during the war and its aftermath.

The eldest of three girls, Thura comes from a close-knit, middle-class Shia Muslim family. Her father, Mouayad, was a professor at Baghdad University who also spent time working for the government. Her mother, Ahdaf, was a scientist until she gave up her career to raise her daughters. Apart from a brief period living in England while her father studied at Reading University, Thura and her sisters – Aula, seventeen, and Sama, seven – have spent their whole lives in Baghdad.

The family had grown accustomed to the economic sanctions designed to strangle Saddam and his regime, but which also meant that ordinary Iraqis could not buy vital goods. Obtaining enough insulin and clean needles for Aula, a diabetic, was a constant source of worry. And Thura had to share her college textbooks with her friends because there were not enough to go around. Her parents, like many Iraqis, were forbidden from travelling abroad after they returned from England.

On the surface, at least, the Al-Windawis' life was comfortable. Their home was roomy, the girls were all well educated and, with the exception of Sama, they all spoke at least some English. But, like all Iraqis, they lived with constant uncertainty about their future. Everyone knew the war was about to begin, but no one knew how it would end. The anticipation was unbearable.

For Thura, the build-up to war became one long goodbye – to friends, relatives, professors and neighbours. No one knew when they would see each other again or what was going to happen. Everyone feared the worst. Aula, in particular, was terrified. She cried a lot and found concentrating on her schoolwork impossible. Sama was too young to understand what might happen, but her family did their best to prepare her without frightening her. And Thura did her best to be strong for the sake of her sisters.

Throughout the fighting and chaos that followed, Thura recorded her thoughts in her diary. She writes about how the family moved around Baghdad and, finally, escaped the bombs by fleeing to the countryside. She writes of her fears for their safety and her own future and, poignantly, of the death of a much-loved childhood friend.

Her writing, particularly during the war itself, reflected the chaos around her as the long days merged into terrifying nights. The original, unedited version of Thura's diary was written in Arabic. Some entries spanned two or three days.

This is the story of the war in Iraq, as seen through the eyes of a girl who was determined that her words should survive, even though the lives of many of those around her were being destroyed.

This is Thura's diary.

2003 Timeline

14 March
Iraqi schools close

18 March
US President George W. Bush gives Saddam and his sons forty-eight hours to leave Iraq or face attack

20 March
Shock and Awe – the bombing of Iraq by US-led troops begins

23 March
Saddam's family are reported to have fled Baghdad

4 April
Saddam International Airport is officially taken by US troops and renamed Baghdad International Airport

4 April
Thura and her family flee to Al-Jadida, north of Baghdad

9 April
US forces enter central Baghdad
Saddam's statue in Paradise Square is brought down

12 April
The Al-Windawis return to Baghdad

23 April
Thura hears about the death of her childhood friend Fahad

30 April
The night-time curfew imposed upon the citizens of Baghdad is lifted

17 May
Thura returns to college

4 June
Thura's twentieth birthday

22 July
It is reported that Saddam's sons Uday and Qusay have been killed

26 August
Thura leaves Baghdad for the University of Pennsylvania in Philadelphia, America

13 December
Saddam Hussein captured by US troops

People and Places

People

Ahdaf Al-Windawi	Thura's mother
Ahmed, Uncle	Thura's uncle on her mother's side
Aida	A family friend; Qusay's wife and mother of Ali, Fahad and Salam
Ali, Uncle	Thura's uncle on her mother's side
As'ad	Thura's mother's cousin
Aula Al-Windawi	Thura's seventeen-year-old sister
Basmina, Auntie	Thura's maternal great aunt; As'ad's mother
Fahad	a family friend, killed during the bombing
Fedaeen	a military group run by Saddam's son Uday
Granny	Thura's maternal grandmother
Hamza	uncle of the Prophet Muhammad
Haydar, Uncle	Thura's uncle on her mother's side
Hussein	Prophet Muhammad's grandson; killed in a battle and an important figure to Shia Muslims
Jabar, Dr	Thura's professor
Jalal Talabani	Kurdish leader
Jasim	Granny's nephew
Jihan	family friend and reporter
Kadhim, Uncle	Thura's eldest uncle on her father's side
Khalil, Uncle	Thura's uncle on her father's side
Lina	one of Thura's best friends
Linus	Thura's friend from college
Masoud Barzani	Kurdish leader
Mazen, Uncle	Thura's uncle on her mother's side
Mounaf	Thura's cousin; Uncle Khalil's son
Mouayed Al-Windawi	Thura's father and a professor at Baghdad University
Mouhamad, Uncle	Thura's uncle on her mother's side; lives in Malaysia
Omar	Thura's cousin; son of Uncle Khalil
Prophet Muhammad	Founder of Islam: birthday 13 May
Qusay	A family friend; Aida's husband and father of Ali, Fahad and Salam

Qusay	Saddam Hussein's son
Rand	Thura's friend
Roula	Thura's friend
Saddam Hussein	President of Iraq
Sama Al-Windawi	Thura's seven-year-old sister
Senan	Thura's cousin; Uncle Khalil's son
Shia Muslim	Thura's family are this type of Muslim
Sunni Muslim	Saddam and his government are this type of Muslim
Uday	Saddam Hussein's son; set up own militia
Umm Jasim	Thura's great aunt and mother of Jasim
Saad Al-Adamy	Thura's father's friend
Zaynab	Thura's friend who went to Syria

Places

Abu Hanifa Mosque	an important Mosque in Baghdad
Adhamiya	the neighbourhood where Thura lives
Al-Alwiya Maternity Hospital	the hospital where Thura was born
Al-Jadida	the area north of Baghdad where Thura's family took refuge during the bombing
Al-Nida'a Mosque	new mosque damaged by tanks
Al-Shamisiya	oldest part of Baghdad
Baratha	a cemetery in Baghdad
Doura	an area south of Baghdad
Jadiriya	a beautiful suburb in Baghdad
Kadhmiya	a district of Baghdad
Kerbala	town one hour's drive from Thura's house
Mahmudiya	district of Baghdad where Uncle Ali's family live
Mosul	a town in northen Iraq
Najaf	town near Baghdad with a big cemetery
Paradise Square	a square in Baghdad
River Tigris	the river that runs through Baghdad
Arasat Al-Hindiya	an area close to Baghdad
Samarra'a	a city north of Baghdad
Sha'ab	district of Baghdad; suffered heavy bombardment during the war

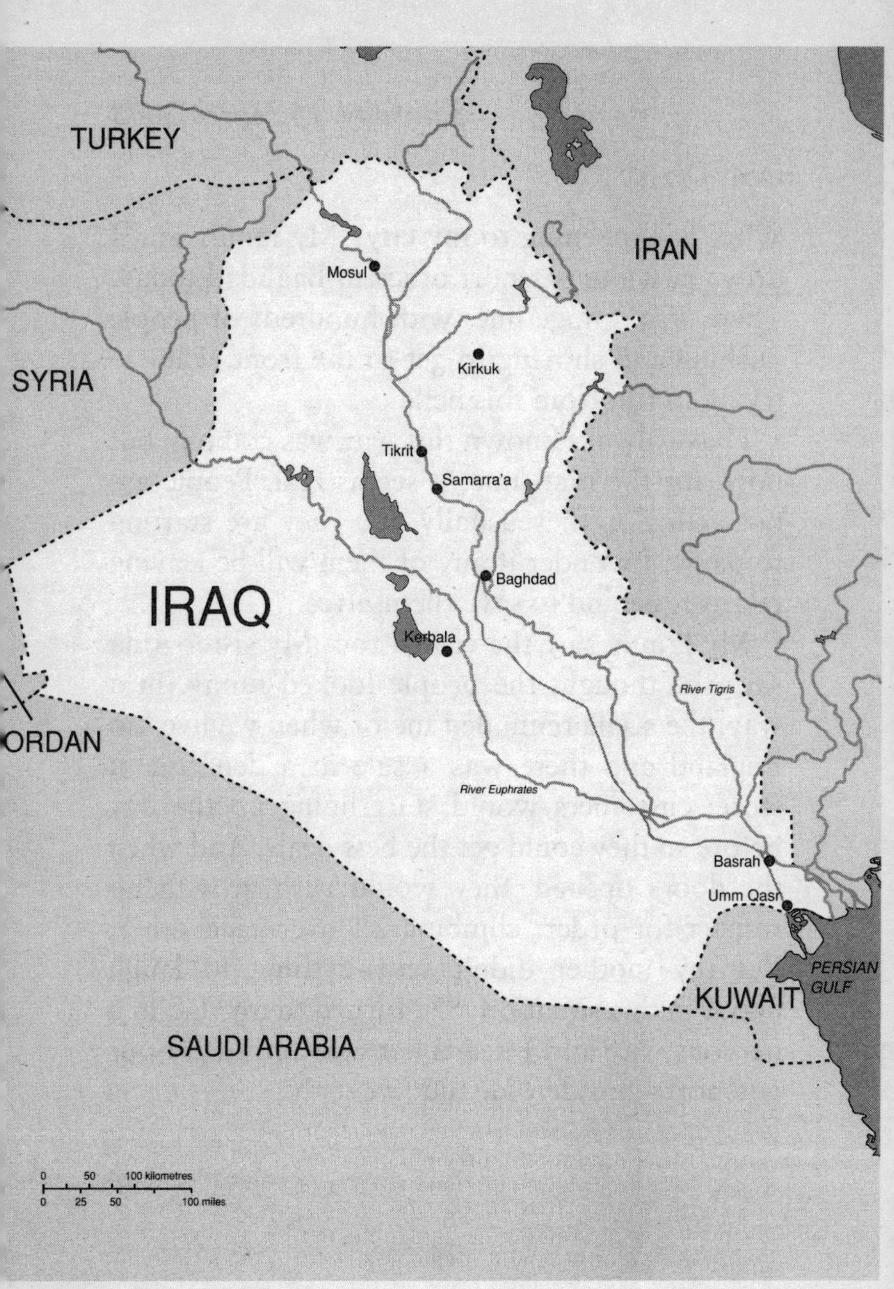
TURKEY
IRAN
SYRIA
IRAQ
ORDAN
SAUDI ARABIA
KUWAIT
PERSIAN GULF
Mosul
Kirkuk
Tikrit
Samarra'a
Baghdad
Kerbala
River Tigris
River Euphrates
Basrah
Umm Qasr
0 50 100 kilometres
0 25 50 100 miles

Saturday, 15 March 2003

Dear Diary,

What is happening to my city? My family and I drove past the passport office in Baghdad today. There was a huge line, with hundreds of people pushing and shoving to get to the front. They're trying to run from this hell.

I have always known this war was coming, but now, for the first time, it seems real. People are not acting as they usually do. They are starting to panic. I wonder if any of them will be leaving relatives behind to save themselves.

My family saw the crowd too. My sister Aula said she thought the people looked funny. In a way, the scene reminded me of when we lived in England and there was a sale at a department store; customers would start lining up the day before so they could get the best deals. And when the doors opened, they would rush in with no respect for order, climbing all over each other. But my mother didn't see anything to laugh about in this situation. She turned to my dad in a nervous way and I heard her ask him to get our passports in order. He did not reply.

Sunday, 16 March 2003

Dear Diary,

Today was a normal day at college. But you can tell from the expressions on the students' faces that they are nervous about the prospect of war. One of my good friends, Rand – who always makes us laugh in class – is terrified of facing war. She does not want to lose anybody in her family and told us that she will cry herself 'to death if I receive news that one of you is missing'.

We don't know exactly when, or even if, the war is going to start, and are hoping that President Bush will withdraw his troops and begin to talk peace. That has been the case every time we have been on the brink of war in past years.

Monday, 17 March 2003

Dear Diary,

Another day, but one with a strange taste. I got up early to start preparing our house, in case war comes. First I gathered together all the valuables on the ground floor of our home. I wrapped the crystal glasses in foam so they won't break if there are explosions and concussion from the missiles. We had to move the furniture too, to protect it. It was very painful and the empty rooms made me feel unhappy; there was no joy or beauty left in them. Our best vases and the sky-blue ashtrays, so heavy I couldn't lift them when I was a child, were all packed away.

This evening we did the laundry. We don't usually wash clothes at night but if there is a war, the water supply is bound to get cut off so Mum said we had to wash everything now. As well as washing the bed linen, clothes and blankets, I washed some of the soft toys I cuddle up to in bed at night: a teddy bear – the colour of a newborn baby – called Pinky that my friend Rosa gave me, and a blue doll, barely larger than my hand, with twinkling eyes and red cheeks that I call Tabby.

Hardly any students turned up at college today because, like me, they were all busy preparing for the days ahead. One of our professors, Dr Jabar, came to see us. There weren't enough of us to have a proper lesson so he just talked. He asked us to share our dreams of the future. I said I would like to find a cure for cancer. A friend said if I did, to let her know and to put my name on it so she would know not to buy it. Everyone laughed. Another friend said he would like to own a medical factory. At the end of his talk Dr Jabar said, 'I hope I will see you soon and that nobody is missing. Good luck to everybody. Maybe I won't be there but remember me.'

Later I sat with some of my friends and played *beatha* – a name game played with fast-moving hands and strips of paper – so we could forget our pain. In the game, our hands end up stacked one upon the other, so we took this as a sign that we would always be together. There are laughs and smiles on our faces. But nobody can see the pain in our hearts.

Saying goodbye to everyone outside college was the saddest moment of my life. Diary, I want to describe to you the meaning of 'goodbye'. It hurts. Whenever I try to stop the tears, I can't prevent them from falling. It makes my throat dry. There's an emptiness inside my chest. It makes my face pale. It makes me ask myself, *Will I see them again . . . in a new life?*

The phone here at home doesn't stop ringing. Everyone's calling everyone else to say goodbye – my friends, my family's friends, relatives – and every call ends with us saying, 'We hope to see you again. Go in peace.' A lot of people have already left Baghdad. My friend, Roula, has gone to a town called Hit in western Iraq – only yesterday she was at college taking pictures of us all with her digital camera – and Zaynab, whose make-up is always so perfect, has gone to Syria.

I don't know, I'm nervous . . . I feel tense . . . I can't breathe because I've been crying so much. I've always hated goodbyes. I'll write more another day. I have a feeling the war is going to start soon. If the air-raid sirens go off I'll know it has really begun.

Tuesday, 18 March 2003

Dear Diary,

So far everything's fine: President Bush has given Saddam Hussein and his sons another forty-eight hours to resign, which means we've got some more time to prepare for the war.

We were hoping to use a shelter at a local school to ride out the bombing. It's one of the few places we could hide. It's just off the playground near the middle of the school. You have to go down two flights of stairs to reach it. As you walk into the shelter it is dark. There are four single bulbs in the roof of a narrow hallway, which has five rooms running off it. But now I'm worried that we will not be able to seek shelter in the girls' school after all, because the headmistress says she's under strict instructions from the Ministry of Education not to let anyone take over the school. Even though Dad begged her to let local people use it she still refused. But if 'silliness is a gift', as they say in our country, then the headmistress proved she's the most gifted of all. How will she be able to face the families who live around here if their children are killed?

Mum decided to go shopping with Dad, but they didn't buy much – just enough for one day. We don't know when the power stations will break down, so there's no point keeping a lot of things in the freezer.

What really upset me today was when I phoned one of my best friends, Lina, to ask if she'd been to the college. She said she had, but that the place had been a pathetic sight; all the labs were closed up today and their contents put into storage, and all the windows have been taped up to stop them shattering if a bomb goes off nearby.

So many of our friends are leaving Baghdad. Omar's gone to Samarra'a, a city to the north. Another friend of ours from college, Linus, has gone to Mosul in northern Iraq – we both belong to a club for Western pop-music fans. The few students who did go to college today all looked sad and anxious about what's going to happen in the next few hours. It broke my heart to hear about it all from Lina. At twelve o'clock the college was closed – two and a half hours early.

My sisters, Aula and Sama, haven't been to class since their schools were closed last Friday, partly because all the parents are worried and partly because the school bus services have been suspended, too.

Baghdad is starting to look depressing to me. The streets are full of demonstrators chanting 'Stop the war!' The shops are all empty and their owners have taken all the big goods away from the shopping district downtown. Some of them have even bricked up their shop windows. The streets are full of barricades. Traffic police are wearing army helmets now and carry Kalashnikov rifles. I've never seen this sort of thing before. I wonder how long it's going to carry on . . . I wish it could all be over as quickly as possible. We've heard rumours that the fighting will only last between one week and ten days. I hope they're true.

Wednesday, 19 March 2003

Dear Diary,

Today was a long day. My mother woke me and said this was the day we had to go to Granny's house until my sisters get used to all the noise of the missiles and explosions and gunfire, and the boom of the planes flying overhead. It'll be scary for the little ones at first, so they've got to be able to get used to it gradually or they'll suffer the effects for a long time afterwards.

We went to the pharmacy today to buy my diabetic sister, Aula, some insulin, but the shelves were empty, and the pharmacist said that insulin is in short supply. We ended up buying six months' worth from four or five different chemists. We also managed to find her blood-test kits and some new needles – a special kind that don't hurt so much when she injects herself. It was very expensive, but we don't care about the money we have to spend to get what my sister needs, because money comes and goes, but who will replace my sister if I lose her? Aula can't eat sweets or chocolate, which she loves so much, because of her illness, and in Iraq you can't buy sweets or sugar-free treats for diabetics. We keep

Aula's insulin in a fridge belonging to a friend of Dad's who's got his own private generator.

As a family we want to be together, but we decided Dad will stay here to watch the house and we – my mother, two sisters and me – will go to Granny's. Aula has been crying. She doesn't want Dad to stay at home alone: she wants him to come with us. But we can't leave the house empty for long periods of time – we might get burgled, or with all the bombing there could be a problem with the water and electricity. This house is all we've got and it wouldn't be easy to replace.

The most secure room in the house is Dad's study, so we helped to prepare the house for him before we left. We pushed his heavy desk in front of the main door so robbers could not come in. Our two dogs, Bambash and Max, went to our neighbour's house.

We packed food, trainers, medicine, face masks (in case of a chemical-weapon attack by either side in the war) and potassium citrate, which you take if you get poisoned by gas.

Dad's promised to come and visit us from time to time. How long are we going to be at Granny's house? I think the best thing is for us to spend tonight there, at least; that way there'll be lots of us all together, so we won't be frightened by the sound of the first missiles falling. Granny will be there and so will four of my uncles with their wives and my cousins. We'll all keep each other's spirits up and we'll feel safer with my uncles around. It'll be easy to keep my little sister, Sama, occupied, too. She'll be able to play with the other children, unaware of the danger all around us.

These are the last hours before the bombing, and everything is changing fast. My friends are all staying home. Some are talking about weapons of mass destruction, and electronic bombs which ruin electricity and water supplies and give people terrible headaches.

I am so worried about these last bombs. Maybe girls who aren't married yet will have trouble getting pregnant because of them. Maybe pregnant women will suffer. I have heard that after these bombs fall, people seem drunk even though they have not been drinking. What will happen to these people?

All the shops and streets are empty. The windows are bricked up. The new ice-cream shop, Penguin, already has broken windows. The government ministries are empty. We are waiting.

I am suddenly seeing things as I never saw them before. This is the hardest day of my life. What am I going to see? People are saying goodbye to each other . . . We are like the *Titanic* going down, drowning in the ocean.

I felt sad as I closed my bedroom door tonight, thinking how much I'm going to miss being able to spend time there and sleep in my own warm, cosy bed. I feel like a writer without pen or paper to express what's going on inside her . . . I hope I get to come back soon.

(Later) The beautiful streets of the capital don't look normal any more. In most squares and at most road junctions, soldiers have taken up positions surrounded by sandbags. On the way to Granny's house I could see people going off to say goodbye to their friends and relations. Others were still stocking up for the war; they looked like little ants laying aside a store of food for the winter. It reminded me of when I last went to the market. The place was packed, and everyone was buying all sorts of things in huge quantities. The stallholders had so many customers they had to serve each one as quickly as they could. People particularly wanted tins of tomato paste – it's a basic ingredient of most Iraqi dishes. Imported goods like dried food, canned things, toothpaste, soap, cotton, tissues and bottled water have started disappearing from the shops. I just hope God will save us and keep us together. I will try to write every day so the world will know what happened here.

Thursday, 20 March 2003
First day of Shock and Awe

Dear Diary,

It's 9.02 p.m. There is shooting outside from the Iraqi army. Saddam Hussein is on TV talking about the missiles dropped on Mosul by British planes. Missiles are also falling in Kuwait. Things are not normal here. The whole family is crowded together in my uncle Ahmed's bedroom at Granny's house, watching TV. We've called my uncle Mouhamad in Malaysia and he gave us some news. He says the Americans ran away from Umm Qasr, a port city in Iraq. Granny said it's bedtime, so me and my mum and sisters have gone into Granny's room.

(Later) Uncle Ahmed, who'd been out, came

back to Granny's and told us that there is a government building burning in the street near Arasat, one of Baghdad's smartest districts. I hear and feel the first missiles exploding – when the earth shakes, your whole body shakes as well. What's going to happen to us? There is only fear in my house. Aula hid herself in Mum's arms because she feared the war. Her face looked scared, her eyes were wide and her body was shaking. Mum tried to calm her down. Sama slept through the whole thing.

A little while later everything went quiet outside, and all of us in Granny's room were silent, too. Granny told everyone to go back to bed. We were all looking at each other calmly but no one said anything, although there were all sorts of questions going through our minds. Everyone looked confused. 'I don't want any of you to be afraid,' Granny said. 'We're going to be hearing noises like these all day, every day, so we'd better get used to them.' We all respect Granny and love her so much. She's a very strong woman. When my grandfather died, she brought up my five uncles and my mother on her own, and she has seen many wars. She kept telling us not to be afraid and to control our tempers, as 'there is so much more to come'.

Uncle Ahmed served as a conscript for years, in the war with Iran during the 1980s. 'Don't be scared,' he said to us, 'it's nothing to worry about. Just a few fireworks going off, that's all.' He knows a lot about missiles, having been a soldier, and he was only trying to cheer us up. But I know perfectly well that the missiles aren't fireworks: they've been sent to kill and destroy, not for fun.

(Later) The B52s came tonight, but they've now accomplished their horrible mission and it's time for bed. I've still got the sound of their engines ringing in my ears. The explosions made an incredible racket, and each time they sent out great gusts of wind that blew the curtains about. Even though it's cold outside, we've left all the windows open because we're afraid the force of the blasts might smash them and send the glass flying into our faces.

I'm in a bed made up on the floor, covered with a thick blanket. I don't know if I'm shaking because of the cold or the fear. I can still feel the pressure of the bombs in my ears. All the children are asleep in the same room. My aunt is watching them so if they wake up they will not be afraid. My uncles are sleeping together and

Granny is ordering everyone around.

Poor Mum is very worried about Dad. I understand how she is feeling but she won't say anything. She doesn't want anyone else to experience what she is going through.

The bombs are starting again. They're falling harder. We just wrap ourselves up in blankets to keep warm, and hope for the best.

Friday, 21 March–Saturday 22 March 2003

Dear Diary,

It's Kurdish New Year. Every year we used to have a picnic, music, dancing. Not this year. This year is the celebration of bombs. Half the capital has been destroyed. All around the city you can see thick smoke from black oil and from missiles. There's a dark cloud over Baghdad.

The alarms begin as early as 8.30 a.m., and we are getting more scared in the house. Today they continued until 11 p.m., and the sound of the missiles is getting louder.

I need to sleep, but I know it will be another difficult night.

The Turkish army wants to join the war in Kurdistan. Maybe this war will take a long time.

The news is confusing from the south. The radio says the Americans are running away from their positions, but sometimes it says the opposite: that they are getting closer to the capital. And the reports say women and children are fighting the Americans.

It is still the first stage for us. I feel sorry for our army: for all those people who will lose their lives. Already so many are dying. Pieces of shrapnel are falling everywhere in the street. There is broken glass. People are beginning to tell us to leave to go to the countryside. We can only say God is with us because we still have water, electricity and the telephone. Every night, we call friends and family after each bomb to see if they are all right.

But the children are so scared! Aula is so afraid of the noise, and every time a plane goes over our house the noise is indescribable – unless you live with it, you cannot know it.

(Later) We are very frightened now. A missile just fell nearby and I literally jumped out of my chair. Sama is scared. She comes and sits on my lap and we watch the windows shake. Mum went back to sleep. This is another long night.

Sunday, 23 March 2003

Dear Diary,

Before I come to anything else, let me tell you more about last night. It was dark and there were constant sounds of explosions and air-raid sirens warning of enemy attacks again and again, each one coming only minutes after the last one had ended. We don't pay any attention to the sirens any more. The planes were passing right overhead – they made a terrifying noise. No one except the children could sleep; the rest of us were all lying awake in bed shivering, but whether from fear or the cold I still don't know.

The scariest thing today was the way some of the planes flew low. The pilots move about with complete freedom because they know that no Iraqi planes are going to stop them. Even so, everyone's sure the Iraqi anti-aircraft fire has succeeded in shooting down some of the enemy planes. People have started searching for the pilots. Saddam Hussein has issued orders offering rewards to anyone who brings down an enemy plane or manages to capture an enemy pilot or destroy a piece of enemy equipment, or who kills enemy soldiers or takes them prisoner.

These are weird orders, don't you think? Are the kind of people willing to give their lives for their country really going to be motivated by silly things like that? But Saddam's had control of the entire state budget for ages now, paying whatever he likes to whoever he likes, however he likes.

Today I spent all my time helping the others to tidy up and clean the house. For days now I've been thinking about the future. In the past I've always enjoyed studying; in a few years I'll be a qualified chemist. But now I feel clouds gathering all around me. Will I really go back to my class? The missiles are destroying everything and the Americans are coming, wreaking havoc along the way. There are still films showing what they did in Vietnam. They won't think twice about using every kind of weapon they've got; President Bush openly said he's prepared to do whatever it takes to win the war.

It's been announced on the state news that the Iraqi First Lady, together with the President's daughters and his sons, Uday and Qusay, have left the country and gone to Syria, accompanied by three lorries.

Hearing this really shocked us. How can they flee to save their own skins after all the ruin and destruction they've brought about? Why are we ordinary people the ones who have to die while they run away?

A bit later this evening, Iraqi TV showed footage of Saddam Hussein in a meeting with a few of his senior aides, as well as his two sons who were sitting beside him. A few years ago Uday set up his own militia, called the Fedaeen, and took personal responsibility for running it and offering financial incentives to anyone who joined up. The militia had all the means of the state at its disposal and no one had the right to interfere in its affairs. One of the most notorious things they did was to publicly behead several young women in the streets. And there he was on TV today, sitting with the army's top brass, discussing the war, when he's never done a day's military service in his life.

Saddam put his younger son, Qusay, in charge of the Republican Guard, which is made up of the Iraqi army's crack troops. And that wasn't all: Qusay was also made responsible for the biggest branch of the intelligence agency in Iraq, the Special Security Service. This is the branch that is responsible for the security of the

President and all the different authorities connected to him. Its agents have to search anyone who goes into the same room as the President, even ministers and other members of the Iraqi leadership. Ordinary people are forbidden to have darkened windows in their cars to keep off the sun, which gets incredibly hot in the summer, and anyone caught breaking this law has their car confiscated. Because of this you can always tell which are the President's cars, as they are the only ones allowed to have darkened windows. Some of them have heavy curtains inside as well, to stop people seeing who the passengers are.

Another night's come round and at Granny's house there's a new fear in the air. The two girls' schools directly opposite have suddenly been taken over by several government and Baath Party organizations, and turned into alternative headquarters. They've abandoned their usual offices because of the likelihood that they'll be bombed. Everything points to the fact that things are going from bad to worse. President Bush has already warned that the coalition forces will hit schools if they're taken over by the army or the Iraqi leadership.

With things as they stand, Granny's decided

we should get ready to leave Baghdad. There's nowhere in Iraq that's completely safe – some places are just safer than others, that's all. Al-Jadida, the area north of Baghdad where Granny's sister, Umm Jasim (which means Jasim's mother) lives, is one of them. We took refuge there during the 1991 Gulf War. It's a little farming village and Umm Jasim's children produce all the eggs and chickens there. The other villagers are all from the same tribe as her husband, and they're known for their hospitality. The area is very green and full of palm trees and orange and lemon groves. The family live in a beautiful, modern house overlooking the River Tigris.

Granny told Uncle Mazen and Uncle Ahmed to go to Al-Jadida immediately and take essential items like bedding, food and water with them. The journey to Al-Jadida was full of danger for Uncle Mazen and Uncle Ahmed; they had to cross through important military zones – liable to be bombed at any moment – and then be back by sundown.

As the hours went by we were all worrying about what might have happened to them on the way. I can't write about what Granny must have been feeling; they're her own children, after all.

But at long last we had the joy of seeing them return, bringing strict instructions that we were to leave immediately, as everyone was waiting for us in the village. It turned out that some of Granny's sisters had already arrived there with their families, and that a house had been set aside especially for Granny and the rest of the family. But eventually she decided that it was still too soon for us to go, because there were so many of us it wouldn't be easy for us all to set off now.

On days like this it's impossible to keep the children cooped up inside for long, but it's also dangerous to let them play out in the open. The only thing we could do was make the most of the fact that there wasn't a power cut; Tom and Jerry cartoons are the best way to keep them glued to the TV. They were laughing as they watched, and we were laughing too. After they'd gone to bed we also let our hair down a bit, although it wasn't the right time to be listening to music: the noise of explosions made it impossible. We had no choice but to watch long Hollywood films. At any rate, we certainly had no desire to watch war films while we were in the thick of a war ourselves.

The eight o'clock news on the Al-Alam

channel showed how the fighting was developing; where it was taking place, how far the American forces had got and what direction they were moving in.

Yet again, the aerial bombardment and the missile strikes are raining down on us. The headquarters of the Iraqi Air Force, less than a kilometre away from our house, has come under a series of attacks. The building looked like it was wobbling. Granny's house keeps shaking too, as though we're in an earthquake. The noise is like thunder. It's scary and I'm frightened . . . Dear Diary, can you tell what I'm feeling, all alone in my bed? I wish I were the same age as my sister Sama, so I could cuddle up to Mum. Talking loudly or laughing doesn't help to shake off the fear any more – there's no let-up in the explosions.

Where's Dad? He hasn't been round all day. Mum can't make any crucial decisions about what the family's going to do without discussing it with him first. She's let me into one of her secrets: she's buried the gold jewellery Dad gave her when they got married in 1982 in the far corner of the back garden. Dad chose the spot. We don't know what might happen, and if anything does go wrong I'll be able to get some use out of it in the future. In my country women always ask for gold jewellery from the man they marry: it's seen as money for the family to use later on, and usually the woman gives the gold back to her husband if he needs it for some project to help the whole family, or in case they ever have financial problems.

I'm less than twenty years old, yet already Mum's started telling me secrets like this – just when she's the one who should be listening to my secrets. Sorry, Diary, let me go to sleep so I can escape from all this horror around me.

Monday, 24 March 2003

Dear Diary,

Today I briefly went back home to get phone numbers of friends. Lina and Wathika are in Adhamiya, where there is a lot of bombing. They said the bombing hit the Mukhabarat, and that glass is everywhere.

Another friend, Abir, called me. She said all our group of friends are gone – some went to suburbs outside Baghdad, some went to their relatives' houses.

We're worried about another friend in Mosul.

I'm most worried about Abir – she lives near Saddam International Airport.

Tuesday, 25 March 2003

Dear Diary,

At last we are back home. I am going to be in my bedroom again. It's so nice to be home sweet home. I think I'll be able to sleep, now that I've calmed down a bit. Some of the young guys who live around here have volunteered to defend the neighbourhood, and they're taking it in turns to keep watch around the clock. They've put sand-bag defences at the street corners, and the Baath Party has supplied them with Kalashnikovs. But all the same, they won't be able to do anything about the noise of the planes and the bombs. It has become like a weird, disturbing kind of music to me.

Wednesday, 26 March 2003

Dear Diary,

During the last few days there have been freak sandstorms here – it's as though Mother

Nature's showing us how angry and hurt she is about the war. The weather's been chopping and changing, and the air has been so thick with red dust from the desert that you can only see a few metres in front of you.

What's made matters worse is that the government's been burning huge amounts of oil inside Baghdad itself, because they think that by sending up clouds of black smoke they can affect the aim of the American missiles. They did the same thing in 1991, except that then they burnt piles of used tyres instead. This time they've dug dozens of ditches in and around the city, then filled them with crude oil and set the oil alight. The air is covered with thick, black smoke. The smell reminds me of the smoke trail that comes off a freshly extinguished match. I can't stand the smell or the way it pollutes the air. At night, as the sun goes down, the sky turns a combination of shades, from deep purples to fire-engine red.

Breathing is so difficult. It feels like you are stuck in a burning building, choking on the fumes. There is no fresh air any more. The leaves on the trees start to wilt. How will we get rid of all this dust and black smoke? Even if it rains, it will rain black drops of water. And it will hurt the soil. Every single living cell will be harmed by this weather. There are no sounds from the birds. Mother Nature is depressed and in pain.

This pollution is what causes lung cancer. I smell the dust and I go to the bathroom to wash my face, hoping maybe I will breathe fresh air. But it doesn't help. Poor Aula and Mum, they are sensitive to the dust. Every two minutes they must blow their noses with tissue. It looks like they are sick. They carry tissues with them wherever they walk. We are drowning in this polluted, black, dusty world.

Mum has finished cleaning the living room that we watch TV in. She also cleaned the kitchen. She had to sponge everything down with a bucket of water to wipe away all the dust, and she had to clean the glasses by hand. We all helped. Each of us has a certain amount of water to use for cleaning. We have a three-gallon bucket each, filled halfway to the top. It came from our rations stored in the bathroom.

Sama was sitting and straightening up her Barbie dolls and teddy bears. We could not clean the whole house, only the ground floor and the bathrooms.

Friday, 28 March 2003

Dear Diary,

Today relatives and friends came to visit us. They are starting to visit a lot because they are worried about us and want to know if we are OK. The phone lines have been cut because the telephone exchange has been bombed. It is getting harder and harder to contact each other and find out exact news.

Saturday, 29 March 2003

Dear Diary,

My dad's friend Saad Al-Adamy and his wife and three children came to visit us. One of the children is only seven months old – just a baby. We tried to stop him being afraid of the noise from the bombs. We took him in our arms and comforted him. His sister Assal is twelve years old, but she is just as scared. I don't want her to be afraid because the bombs are everywhere all the time. And it is getting worse. She is starting to understand that, and she is better than when I last spoke with her on the phone. Her older brother, Sayef, is sixteen and understands the whole situation. But they are still children. And it's difficult to take care of children during a war. It's hard to control them at night, and during the day they like to go out; they like to play. Now they have to stay inside the house. They cannot play, they cannot see friends a lot – it's not easy.

Just as every other day, the dust is everywhere. It's as if we didn't do any cleaning yesterday. But today there is more. I feel sorry for Aula and Mum – they are still sneezing. We didn't clean the whole house today, just the living room, kitchen and sitting room. Mum said we would have to wait to get rid of all of it.

Although I took my shower yesterday, I feel the dust all over me, on my hair, on my body. And because water is so precious, it's important that I only use a little amount of it, just to wash over myself to get off this dust. I would usually have a good bath, but not now. I use a quarter of the water I would normally use. Mum has difficulties washing the dishes. There are so many guests and visitors coming to our house and she has hardly any water to wash up after them.

How I wish all this dust would stop. It's getting boring, so boring. I just hope that it will stop soon.

Granny came. She was very worried about us after she heard from my aunt that we still hadn't left Baghdad. The troops are getting closer all the time. Granny's face was full of panic. She and my uncle Haydar came as fast as they could to see how we were. They couldn't call because the phones aren't working. She was relieved that she had come and that we hadn't been harmed.

Because they were here, and because there was no water at their house, they had a bath. Granny told us it was a very good thing that we had left her apartment because the bombardment there was very heavy and very frightening. The Al-Alwiya Maternity Hospital, where I was born, was damaged; it must have been terrifying for the mothers and babies inside. In some way, somehow, it is quieter here.

Dad decided we should go and see my uncle Khalil who lives in our neighbourhood in an area called Al-Shamisiya, which is one of the oldest parts of Baghdad. Our families are very close. Uncle Khalil and his family have decided that they're not leaving their house under any circumstances, even though they're in an incredibly dangerous position, because a lot of weapons have been hidden in nearby palm groves.

My three cousins, Omar, Mounaf and Senan,

are all teenagers but they were obviously terrified. Omar is older than me, and when I look at him I see a very strong man, but he and his brothers have in some way been affected by the storming bombardment near their house. Now, every time there is the slightest noise outside, they think it is a missile or a plane coming. The family all sleep in the dining room because it'll be the safest place if the windows get broken in an explosion. But Omar doesn't sleep, he lies awake waiting for the nightmare to begin; the coming of tons of missiles. But my uncle's not the sort to fuss about things like that, and he insists on sleeping in his own bedroom upstairs. The real problem is his wife, Afaaf; she gets into a complete panic if so much as a cockroach gets into the house. She was beside herself with worry when the bombing started – because of the insects that might come into the house if the windows broke! Dad advised her to go to the shelter in her neighbours' basement, but her reply was hilarious. 'I can face the American missiles,' she said, 'but I couldn't sleep in that shelter if there was an insect in it.'

Uncle Khalil told Dad that their elder brother Kadhim, who's seventy years old now, has decided not to leave his house, even though the rest of his family have all gone to Syria. The problem is that his house is only a stone's throw away from some palaces belonging to Saddam's family and his half-brother Barzan. If Kadhim really does stay in his house it's sure to be the end of him; the palace complex has already come under attack, and it's bound to again. Kadhim refuses to go to the shelter under his house because he's convinced there won't be anyone to get him out if he does. So, instead, he's decided to take shelter in his garden, under a roofed area made out of concrete. 'If you don't find me, you'll know I've died over in that corner,' he said to my uncle. So far he's all right, thank God.

This evening we came back home again. Like my cousins, we were fed up with all the nationalistic songs they keep repeating on Iraqi TV. The Iraqi army leaders only ever talk about their victories, but I don't believe a word of it – their propaganda's just the same as it was during the first Gulf War, even though things are completely different now. This time it's a battle for the control of Iraq by the greatest power the world has ever known, with all the latest technology at its disposal. I keep wondering: *What will happen in the end?*

Sunday, 30 March 2003

Dear Diary,

Today was a really sad day. The Doura district in south Baghdad came under attack from cluster bombs. We've got quite a few friends who live there, as well as one of my other cousins and his family. We were all so worried about them, but we couldn't phone or go to see them, because the area's considered so dangerous at the moment.

On TV they've been showing children who've been taken to hospital with terrible burns. I had tears pouring down my face as I watched, wondering if such terrible things could happen to me, or any of the people I love. They are doing surgery on people without painkillers or anaesthetic. How must that hurt! If you touch a pineapple or a rose thorn, you feel pain. If you fall from a bicycle and get injured, you feel pain. How would it be if you broke your arm, or cut yourself badly? There are men and children dying, and women crying for them. What kind of hatred must they be feeling for the invaders whose leaders say they've sent in their armies to liberate us? And what kind of hatred for the Iraqi leadership as well, which refused, right to the end, to reach a peaceful solution to the problem with the coalition forces.

I see people crying, houses destroyed. One family had lost their house, their car, everything! Those poor people. Where are they going to live now? How can a person live without a home, without clothes, without food, without drink? People do not deserve this.

Monday, 31 March 2003

Dear Diary,

My mum usually sits in front of the TV, watching the news to find out what's going on. Aula sometimes sits with Sama and me, and other times, because she fears the bombs, she sits hiding herself in Mum's arms. Most of the time Sama stays with me. She always wants to be beside me and even tries to act like me. People always say she is the photocopy of me.

The anti-aircraft guns keep blasting away day and night, but they inflict more damage on the people down below than they do on the coalition planes. A four-year-old boy was killed by some shrapnel while he was out playing in front of his house; poor little thing, to get killed by his own people – and his poor mother to have lost her child, too. I feel heartbroken for both of them.

A car that was parked in our street exploded and caused a huge fire when a bit of shrapnel hit its petrol tank. All of this has driven Dad to insist that Sama wears something that looks like a motorbike helmet whenever she wants to go and play in the garden.

There's nothing for me to do these days. I've had plenty of time to study for college and I've been doing some drawing, as well as writing this diary. I've been spending lots of time watching cartoons with Sama too – she especially likes *The Little Mermaid* and *Snow White*. We taped most of them when we were living in England.

Our generator has been a godsend during these difficult times, because it's powerful enough to give us light at night. Occasionally Sama cuddles up to me when she's scared – particularly when big explosions make the windows rattle. I've also been feeling frightened. Sometimes there are whole series of explosions that are so powerful they make us all spring up and go running out of the house, for fear that it might fall down on us.

Mum's problems are going from bad to worse. The water pressure is very weak now, and sometimes it gets cut off altogether. I often

Thura when she was one-and-a-half years old.

Baby Thura and her proud parents, Mouayad and Ahdaf, in Glasgow, 1985.

Thura enjoying a day out in Hyde Park, London.

In the garden at their home in Reading, 1986.

The birthday girl gets a surprise at her nursery school in Wokingham, 1987.

Thura (right), Aula and their father are visited by colleagues from his university.

The family celebrate the award of Mouayad's PhD from the University of Reading, 1989.

Thura plays dress-up in her father's cap and gown.

Thura (left) and Aula enjoy an English funfair.

Thura (far right) with her friends from secondary school, 1999.

Thura (left) and her friend Farah the night before the end-of-year pharmacology exam, 2001. Sama has also finished nursery school.

Thura taking a break from her studies.

Thura (second from left) and her first-year pharmacology classmates.

Thura (right), and her friends Farah (left) and Saada.

Thura in Baghdad, August 2003.

Thura is confident about the future.

find myself wondering whether I'll be able to go back to college soon. But no one knows what the future holds.

War seems to be a fertile breeding ground for rumours, because there are lots of them going around at the moment. The strangest one I've heard is that Saddam's got some American-made nuclear weapons, which he got hold of when the Iraqi army invaded Kuwait, and that he's planning to use them. Dad laughed when he heard this. 'What's he waiting for, then?' he said. 'Don't believe a word of it – Saddam hasn't got anything of the kind. How could he, when the UN weapons inspectors have searched everywhere – even under his wife's pillow?'

The Americans are still engaged in heavy fighting on the outskirts of Najaf and Kerbala, which is one hours drive from where we live. All the roads to both cities have been cut off, so now people can't even bury their dead in Najaf, which has one of the largest cemeteries in the world. People like to be buried there to be close to the tomb of Ali bin Abi Talib, the Prophet Muhammad's son-in-law; all my ancestors are buried there, too. Instead, people are having to bury their dead at home and on open ground, in the hope that they'll be able to dig up the bodies later on and bury them properly in Najaf.

For the last few hours it's been difficult to receive Iraqi radio or TV properly, because the Radio and Television Building has been bombed. Now the Iraqis have started broadcasting from mobile studios to avoid being bombed all over again, but the signal is weak. The Satellite Television Centre has also been destroyed – that was after the pictures of the American prisoners of war were shown on TV. I saw three of them. Two were men but to my astonishment one of them was a woman. How could the Americans send women to fight in a war? I couldn't believe my eyes when I saw her on the screen.

A few hours before the war started, all the journalists staying near the Republican Palace in the western part of the city, moved to the eastern part, where the Palestine Meridien and the Sheraton hotels are. All the foreign correspondents were following the movements of the American and British journalists, on the assumption that they were better informed about when the war was going to start.

Just before the end of the day, news came in that the Americans were in control of Arasat

Al-Hindiya, which is very close to Baghdad. The Iraqi news has also been talking about how a poor Iraqi peasant managed to shoot down an American Apache helicopter with his old rifle. They showed the helicopter on TV: it was still in one piece, but both the pilots had been taken prisoner.

Before I went to sleep, I heard Mum talking to Dad about how the price of tomatoes has gone up, because the tomato farms in Basra have been destroyed, and the ones in Najaf and Kerbala can't get their produce to the capital any more. Dad thought it was for another reason to do with the exchange rate of the dinar against the dollar. But whatever the explanation, it looks as though we'll have to face the prospect of rising prices now – after surviving 'Shock and Awe'. And I've got to think about the next step too, because the time's come for us to leave the house, now that the Americans are on our doorstep.

Tuesday, 1 April 2003

Dear Diary,

Today is April Fool's Day, but now's not the time for jokes. I saw a coffin being brought into the neighbourhood, covered with an Iraqi flag. Everybody was looking outside wondering if it was a relative of theirs – their son or their husband or their brother. Every day we're losing someone because of this war. They are showing films on the TV about the war between the Iranians and the Iraqis. They show how people get killed, and how they lose their arms and their legs, and how they suffer. They show the bodies in the desert. All these are innocent people who get involved in war. They die because of people with big egos who are looking for power. Innocent people have to kill each other for this reason; this stupid reason.

A few hours before the war started, a number of Iraqis who had been taken prisoner during the war with Iran were allowed to return home. One of them was the husband of Aula's teacher, who'd spent twenty-one years in Iranian prisoner camps (which must be some kind of record). When he left, his children were little, and now he's come home to find them all working as doctors and engineers – and not only that, but he's also in the thick of a war that's even worse than the one he fought in all those years ago. Unfortunately for him his house is close to important areas that have come under heavy bombing. As for the prisoners that have been taken in this war, I don't think they'll be gone for long. It's already obvious that the war's going to be short.

One thing that's been happening lately is that whenever the bombing starts, dozens of people go to the mosques and call out Allah's name and shout 'God is great' from the tops of the minarets right until the attacks are over. Everyone can hear them, and we all find it reassuring – it gives us the feeling that God's watching over us. We don't go, though. We're too frightened of going out at night because of the bombardment. We don't go out much during the day because of the missiles. Shrapnel could fall on our heads, or maybe we'd be walking along the street and a missile would fall. Better to stay at home and pray.

Last night, the presidential palace near our house got bombed again. There was an enormous explosion and, because it was so nearby, Aula woke up with a fright. There was only me next to her, and she was absolutely terrified. All I could say was, 'Put your head under the sheet and go back to sleep, and try to forget about what's going on outside if you can.' I was trembling with fear myself and my heart was racing, and I couldn't go back to sleep for ages.

At eight o'clock in the morning Mum told everyone to get up. Then she listened to what they were saying on the news about the way the war was going. No one pays any attention to what the politicians are saying any more.

After breakfast we all went shopping. We bought some vegetables, tomatoes, cucumber and some important things for cooking. We bought a small amount of meat – just enough for lunch and dinner. Other people were going in order to buy only small amounts of food, too. They are like Fear People: shocked expressions on their faces and in a hurry just to get what they need before returning home to wait for another missile strike. Kids were looking in the air, listening for missiles and trying to spot the planes in the sky. They are scared, but for them it is the first time they've seen military planes. Everyone is suspicious of other people's behaviour, worried that it might make somebody target the area and they will get shot.

The house isn't always a depressing place to be. Lots of Dad's friends come to see us, and have some of Mum's excellent Turkish coffee.

At long last Dad agreed for us to get out our secret weapon that was banned by Saddam: our satellite dish! For eight years we'd hidden it in Mum's wardrobe. Unfortunately, when we got it out it seemed to be broken. If we'd been caught with it before, broken or not, Dad would have been sent straight to prison.

The Sha'ab district came under heavy bombardment this morning, in an area close to a busy junction surrounded by shops and houses. There were lots of civilian casualties. The news got out, but the American military spokesman tried to wriggle out of giving an explanation. There aren't any important military, or even civilian, installations in the area to try and hit. No one knows why it was bombed. I can't tell what's true and what isn't any more; the Americans say they want to get rid of Saddam, but they're also killing innocent civilians. Their forces are only a stone's throw away from Baghdad now.

Today on the news they've been repeating the contents of letters sent by Saddam to the Kurdish leaders, Masoud Barzani and Jalal Talabani, warning them against collaborating with the Americans. It seems a bit late to me, to be writing to them about that. Both men have decided to settle old scores with Saddam, but it's the Iraqi people – Arabs and Kurds alike – who'll be the real losers.

Wednesday, 2 April 2003

Dear Diary,

Last night was one I'll never forget. I can hardly bring myself to describe it. In the middle of the night we were thrown out of our beds by some massive explosions. With the whole city in pitch-darkness, no one knew what was happening. The explosions were coming from somewhere nearby, most probably the rail depot, or else some large warehouses belonging to the President's palaces. Some of the missiles flew over our house and we could see the huge flashes light up the sky when each one hit, followed by the deafening sound of the explosions and a great gust of wind. We also heard glass shattering nearby, and at the time we thought some of the windows of our own house had broken, too.

We all got up except for Sama, who was too scared and asked me to stay next to her. Just as

Mum was hurrying to open all the doors of the house, another explosion went off, making the house shake and the lights jiggle about; I had the feeling the roof was about to fall in on us. We were all rooted to the spot, looking at each other wondering what was going to happen next, when the third missile fell. The next few minutes seemed like hours, with the house rocking as more and more explosions came – it's quite old, and who knows if it can take all these tremors? Eventually everything quietened down again, but it took us all a long time to go back to sleep.

In the morning we noticed some cracks in the ceiling, but not big enough to worry about at the moment. We heard that all the warehouses nearby had been completely destroyed, and a lot of new cars that had been hidden in them had been blown up and were now scattered all over the road in little bits.

I've heard that the Americans are fighting near the airport. It came as a big shock to us all to find out that they'd reached the city already. Dad saw some Iraqi soldiers in the street, including a young guy who lives nearby, who told him they'd been ordered to collect anti-tank grenades and go and kick the Americans out of the airport. Dad told him they wouldn't stand a chance and warned him to be careful. The other man interrupted him, 'Do you really think I'm going to go?' he said. 'Our commanders just give orders – they don't go with us, or even tell us how to get there, or how long we'll be there or who's going to bring us food supplies.'

There are more and more dead and injured all over Iraq. A friend of ours had half his house destroyed in the bombing, and couldn't find anyone to help him get his relatives' bodies to a hospital. He filmed them using his video camera, and then buried them himself in the garden in the hope that one day someone will be able to come and move them.

This evening Baghdad looked completely different to me. The streets are still full of dirt from the sandstorms, there are fewer people out than usual and the shops are all closed. The whole city is in darkness because of the oil fires, which you can smell everywhere. Maybe they're a kind of reminder to us of what this war's really about.

We cooked our food on an oil lamp so we can keep our gas for more important things like boiling water. We had our dinner very early. Usually we have it later but we wanted to eat before the bombardment started again. Sama tries to walk around in the darkness and we try to make her sit down. She won't listen so we have to grab her hand, just to make sure she dosen't fall down or have an accident. It is so hard to keep everything under control, from darkness to sunlight, from the house to Dad, from Aula to Mum. Everyone is just drained and worried, and we don't know what to do. Sometimes we forget where the candles are or have to search for a match just to have light. And then when we find each other again, we sit down together, just waiting and waiting and waiting. Overhead it's raining, not water but missiles, and we wonder when the rain will stop.

Thursday, 3 April 2003

Dear Diary,

I don't know where to start. Everything's changing so quickly. Normal life is coming to an end. For the second day in a row thousands of people have been leaving the city. They bring cars to put all their stuff in, everything they need including their water and dried food. They are boarding up their houses and putting chains over their doors. They put locks on these chains, making sure there will be no way a thief can get in. Then they leave. Day after day, hour after hour, a family leaves and another house is empty. They are all running away from this war that is coming to Baghdad. There is fear in our hearts and panic in our minds, just like in 1991. It's hell and there is no way to get away from it except to leave the city.

The affluent parts of the city are deserted – the people who live there were among the first to go, either to neighbouring countries or else to their country houses. But the poor areas are still packed with people. My family aren't rich or poor. In the past we couldn't leave the country because Dad is not allowed to travel, and Mum didn't want to leave him on his own.

At lunchtime we went to see Granny and found her beside herself with worry. Her eldest son Ali and his wife haven't been back to her place since yesterday. They went to check out their flat, which is in the Mahmudiya district, close to a big housing estate for people who work in the army factories. There's been fighting near there. This morning Granny sent two of her sons to go and see Ali, but they couldn't reach his place because the road was closed. Dad tried to put Granny's mind at rest, reminding her that

Ali and his wife had left their daughter with her, so she should try to stay calm. They're probably just stuck in their flat, waiting for the right moment to come back to Granny's house.

Meanwhile, on TV they've been showing civilians in hospital injured in bombing raids while they were driving. We heard about a little girl who'd been hit by shrapnel. She didn't know what had happened to her parents, because the ambulance had brought her to hospital on her own.

Before sunset we went back home. On the way we noticed lots of policemen and armed guards outside public buildings, but apart from them we didn't see any soldiers about. When night fell there was a total blackout all over Baghdad because of a power cut. No one knew what had caused it, but maybe it was to allow the army to move around the city secretly. Dad went out into the garden to start up the generator. A whole series of explosions started going off, but they sounded different this time; I heard Dad say they were tank shells, which meant the war would be over soon. The fighting is so close that we're not safe here any more – we've got to get ready to leave, but not while it's still pitch-dark. And anyway, we can't drive at a time like this.

The bombardment is really freaking us out. The sound is so loud you know the explosions are very near. It's like when you go inside an elevator and it shoots to the top floor – you get a weird, sickly feeling in your stomach. When each bomb drops, you get that feeling and you try to swallow it so you can listen for the next one. It's too loud and too scary. You don't know what to do. You see people in their windows. Everyone is inside their houses, being together. We are always together. We cannot leave each other because it's too scary. Your heart beats so fast. Your eyes are wide open. We are all staring at each other. Dad doesn't know what to do and neither does Mum. Mum is looking for something to do. Then they start to discuss their plans with each other, in very low voices so we cannot hear. Just that we have to leave. It is so sad. This is the third time. How many more times? Why do we have to go from place to place just for safety? Where is a place that we can stay and not be harmed? A place that is quiet? It has to be the countryside. We have no choice.

We were sure this was the right decision after our neighbour's relatives came to their house. They came in a small bus. There were lots of people inside it, running away from another part of Baghdad. They said the tanks were there. All they took with them was what they needed. Some were wearing pyjamas. Some had suits over their bedclothes. They said, 'We cannot go back because there is so much damage. Cluster bombs are falling on people. We have just left everything. We were just concerned for ourselves.'

All of us are very worried about Uncle Ali. Where is he right now? With the bombardment getting harder, what has happened to him? We started to think the worst – things we didn't even want to think, like: *Is he dead?* Maybe he's injured. Maybe he is OK and has just got stuck somewhere. Dad keeps saying that if nothing has happened to him, he will come walking back. This is the way of life. The most important thing is that his child is still with my Granny. The bombardment is everywhere. We don't know who is living and who is dead. As more bombs drop, more people are dying – you just don't know how many.

Dad told us to get everything ready to leave early in the morning, so that we can be in Al-Jadida by lunchtime.

With the help of a few lights powered by the generator, we started packing. Mum had already decided what we were going to take – most importantly, comfortable clothes and shoes, like trainers, and sheets and blankets for the beds. We also packed big black cloaks to wrap ourselves up in – they're what women traditionally wear in the Iraqi countryside, where we're going to be staying. Apart from that we packed some fizzy drinks and sweets, mostly for Sama, and a pot to boil water from the river in. We hid our jewellery inside one of Sama's teddy bears.

Mum looked worried and upset; she was obviously scared about what might happen to us, especially given that we're all so young. She must have been frightened for her own sake, too. She kept asking Dad what could have happened to her brother Ali and his wife.

We all decided to sleep in the same room that night, while Dad sat outside to keep watch in front of the house.

At the moment I'm sitting up in bed writing. I'm so worried – not just for me, but for all my family and my friends from college. They're scattered all over Baghdad, and now the fighting has started in the city. The area we're going to tomorrow won't necessarily be safe, either – it's only ten kilometres away from the army bases north of Baghdad, and there'll probably be lots of missiles and other weapons hidden in the palm groves there. So who knows, we might have to abandon that place suddenly as well.

Friday, 4 April 2003

Dear Diary,

Last night we didn't sleep. The air was full of fumes from the bombs. My head was on the pillow but I was not comfortable inside the room. Sleeping together, there is no space and we were all looking around and listening for each bomb. How far away are they? How *near*? It makes me terrified, always thinking, *Am I going to live or am I going to die?* We didn't know if we were going to live or die last night.

When the first light from the sun appeared, we starting packing up the car. We usually sleep in on Fridays, because for us it's the start of the weekend. It's also a special day for Muslims, because it's the day when we go to pray in the mosque – like Christians go to church on Sundays, and Jews go to the synagogue on Saturdays. But this Friday was different. It only took half an hour to get everything inside the car. We needed to leave as fast as we could.

What were we going to do about our dogs? We couldn't take them with us. After thinking about it Dad decided to leave them at home, once he'd made sure the family who live opposite us could look after them. We've got a huge shaggy guard dog called Max, who stays on the roof terrace; he gets on well with the neighbours. We gave them some money for his food and left him plenty of water, too. The funny thing is that Max, who looks big and brave, has been just as frightened by all the explosions as we have: whenever they start, he hides in a corner and doesn't make a sound.

Our other dog, called Bambash, is smaller; we found him lost near Granny's house one day. We could see he was clever and well trained, and sure enough he has an amazing ability to understand things. He always eats the same food that we do, but he's not allowed to come inside the house while Mum and Dad are praying. That's because Muslims have to wash in a special way before saying their prayers, and we believe that if you touch a dog you're not clean any more. Bambash guards the front door to the house and he never lets cats or strangers in – he and Max only have to bark to scare off burglars. But we noticed that whenever the missiles were falling

Bambash wanted to come inside, so in the end we reached a compromise and gave him a pillow to hide under in his basket, but kept the basket itself outside. The poor little thing used to tremble all over – we could tell how scared he was by the noise of the explosions, looking around trying to understand what was happening.

Dad wasn't too worried about the house getting burgled while we were away, because there are plenty of places in the wealthier parts of the city for people to break into now. All the same, as we left the house Mum recited part of the Koran, which we believe protects our home with God's blessing. It was so sad – it all brought back memories of 1991 for us.

On the way to the main road we stopped by Uncle Khalil's place to tell him we were going, and drop off a set of keys to the house so that he can go and check up on it, or even stay there if he wants to. After leaving his place we found ourselves stuck in the most enormous traffic jam; everyone was heading north out of Baghdad. Normally there would be four lanes of traffic in the road, but now there were seven long lines of all sorts of vehicles. The weather was boiling and completely suffocating – made worse by all the exhaust fumes from the cars, which were crawling along extremely slowly. As we went through the Sha'ab district we could see the bomb damage to all the shops and houses. I wrote about all that before, but it's one thing to write about it and another thing to see it in real life. There were also pieces of black material hung everywhere with the names of people who'd been killed on them.

The vehicles on the road were all packed with people and their luggage – the boots were full of all sorts of cooking things and bedding in particular. Some people were even travelling on the roofs of buses, and everyone was taking eggs with them – probably because they don't go bad too quickly. Lots of cars had bread ovens in them. One thing I'll never forget was the sight of a family who'd crammed themselves and all their possessions into the back of a rubbish truck. What would have happened if there'd been a cluster bomb attack like the one in Doura? There would have been a complete massacre. Dad deliberately drove along the side of the road so that we could jump out and try to save ourselves if anything like that happened.

We had to get through several more traffic jams before we could get away from the residential parts of the city. After that we had to pass through big military zones belonging to the Iraqi army. We saw dozens of tanks heading towards Baghdad, but there were also a lot of old ones that had broken down and been abandoned by the side of the road. There were masses of soldiers as well, standing around outside their bases – presumably because they thought the bases themselves were likely to get bombed – and anti-aircraft guns everywhere.

The drive to Al-Jadida would normally take thirty minutes, but after an hour in the car we still hadn't got far. We were all sweating – not just because of the heat, but because of the danger, too. Dad was smoking like a chimney, so we had to ask him to stop and turn on the air-conditioning.

The journey took us two hours in all, but it was nice when we got there. Lots of other families were already there – some of them had been there since the first day of the war, and the others had gradually followed as they felt the situation in Baghdad get more serious. They welcomed us with open arms, saying, 'It's good that you are alive. We were so worried about you. You have to stay here.'

It feels really safe in Al-Jadida. There are no sounds of bombs or screaming. You see flowers.

The air is very pure. I feel sunlight. I feel everything is normal. People are working. People are all together. Families have smiles on their faces. I don't fear bombs when they are so far away because you cannot feel the effect of it. If I listen hard enough you can hear explosions, and maybe the windows shake a little, but these do not scare us because we have lived in something so much worse.

Dad was completely exhausted: he hadn't slept a wink since yesterday morning, so he went to lie down. The rest of us went to chat to all the women and girls, and Sama went to play with the other children in the garden. My cousins and relatives all asked what it was like: whether the palaces were damaged, how much damage there was and why we stayed in Baghdad for so long. The reason my family had been able to bear the danger in the city was that we'd been so well prepared in advance. And in any case, we love our home and we weren't in a hurry to leave it.

The house we are staying in has got a satellite dish, so we'll be able to follow the news and see all kinds of channels. Four families in total are staying in Granny's nephew Jasim's house, and another five families are staying in the house next door, which belongs to his brother Ali. Granny and the people who've been living with him are going to stay in Jasim's sister's place, and lots of other relatives – mostly Mum's aunts and their families – are staying in other houses, having left everything behind in Baghdad.

In the afternoon Granny and the others arrived. We all rushed out to greet them and ask her what was going on. She said that until now my uncle still had not come back from his flat. Something must have happened to him. My mum was shocked. She almost cried because he is her brother. Then my dad somehow controlled the situation and told them not to worry. He would come back.

We all tried our best not to show our worry to his little daughter, so she wouldn't be upset. We encouraged her to play with the other kids so she had no idea of what was going on. It made me think about what would happen to her if her parents were killed. How would she grow up? Who would take care of her? It is a great responsibility, taking care of a child, especially in such circumstances and especially a young girl; a girl is a big responsibility. What about her schooling? There are other kids everywhere losing their parents, losing their families. How will they grow up? Who will feed and look after them so they can have an ordinary life? It's all getting complicated.

They say that Baghdad is almost empty. Nobody is living there and the streets are so silent you can hear a pin drop. The shops are closed, even the grocery shops, and so I don't know how people get their food. Water is being cut, too. They say that we left just at the right time because the bombs have started to get heavier during the day. It is now a very dangerous place, even the route from Baghdad to the countryside.

We have heard about two women who have sacrificed themselves for their country. For us, this is a new thing. We've never heard of that before – women sacrificing themselves, fighting for their country, their land, their people. I believe that in a war, women must be strong if they lose a son or husband. But I don't believe women should fight. I have never understood why women go into the military in other countries. Women are best at giving love and kindness, not killing.

Saturday, 5 April 2003

Dear Diary,

Last night I slept properly for the first time in ages. The village where we're staying is in a beautiful place beside the River Tigris. There are lots of orange and lemon groves and wonderful, tall palm trees, too – it's as if nature has been untouched here. The way of life in the village is quite typical of the Iraqi countryside. The women do all the housework, and other things too, like milking the cows and making bread the same way it's been done for hundreds of years. The girls do all the laundry by hand, and they also help their mothers out. They're not allowed to have further education, and they usually get married off as soon as they reach their teens – mostly to cousins and other relatives.

I went for a lovely walk through the orchards and then helped collect the eggs from the field that belongs to Jasim's family. The men of the family manage the egg business, and they're pleased because the price of eggs has gone up a lot recently due to shortages.

On the way back I saw a small pool by the river where I played with my cousins in 1991 when I was just a young kid. I remembered how happy we were, just playing and having fun, not realizing what was really going on. Now we are all grown up and we cannot go back to that time. Everything has changed and we now understand, but when you get older sometimes you wish you didn't because you miss all the fun. I saw bushes where we played hide-and-seek and all the memories came rushing back, then they disappeared. Things change too fast. This was only a few years ago but it seems so long.

This evening an officer from the secret services came to the village to see his family. One of my relatives heard that he and his colleagues have been given a holiday. How do soldiers get holiday at a time like this? It's a time for fighting, a time for war, not a time for rest. There is something very strange going on. It's like they are giving up on the war. Things are not going as we think.

It is weird that he has left his office, left his position to go to the countryside with his family. Who gave him this holiday? From where? We know that people cannot take a holiday without permission from the 'headmaster'! Well, maybe the 'headmaster' is not there. Maybe the 'headmaster' has taken a holiday, too. It's really weird!

To our huge relief Uncle Ali and his wife arrived tonight. They were both completely exhausted; they'd been trapped in their home while the fighting was going on in south Baghdad, but last night the Americans moved on. They were the first members of our family to see the Americans. 'They were just as scared as we were,' Uncle Ali said. 'All we had to do was avoid making any sudden movement that might make them suspicious, or else they might think we were suicide bombers and open fire on us – that was what we were afraid of more than anything. In Mahmudiya we saw the bodies of Iraqi soldiers lying in the streets.'

Ali's daughter was the happiest of all of us. She was clapping, saying, 'My dad has arrived! My mum is here!' and they had brought her clothes, which made her even happier. She usually has a pale face, but it wasn't pale any more. She was jumping around. It was so nice to see.

A little while later we decided to celebrate and give thanks to God by killing a lamb and giving the meat to the different families. In my culture, sacrificing a lamb in the name of God is a tradition after something good has happened to a family.

Later on, Mum and Dad decided to go back to Baghdad tomorrow morning to see the dogs and make sure the house is all right, and turn off the water and electricity supplies in case the house gets damaged in the bombing.

Sunday, 6 April 2003

Dear Diary,

This morning was beautiful, with a clear sky and the smell of blossoms everywhere. There aren't any oil fires here, thank goodness. Everyone helped prepare breakfast; cooking here is a group effort, with all the women taking part. Mum's considered the best cook of all, so she's in charge of deciding what we're going to have and how it should all be cooked. We are glad about this because we know when we will get food we like! Dad was especially pleased! It was also a good opportunity for the girls who've only recently got married to learn some recipes.

As for me, the city girl, I had to learn how to bake bread the old-fashioned way. It was a new experience for me. I was taught by a girl called

Aly'a, who's twenty-one years old and married to her cousin with two children already. She first learned to bake bread when she was fourteen years old. I couldn't believe she was so young when she first started doing this. I am nineteen now and I'm not very good! Instead of round loaves, mine sometimes looked like triangles or as if they had faces. I kept burning my arms on the hot oven, too. But it was fun and it passed the time. I was so bored with nothing to do, and so doing the baking with Aly'a kept me amused and it meant I was helping everyone.

Mum and Dad went to Baghdad with Uncle Ahmed this morning, and I was left in charge of looking after my sisters. They told me that on the way back to the village, they saw some planes flying overhead again. On the ground hundreds of soldiers were running for cover all over the place. There were no other cars on the road apart from Dad's, and just as he was approaching a bridge over the Tigris the soldiers started shouting, 'Where are you going? Stop! Turn back! The Americans are on the bridge!' Dad turned the car round and quickly headed back to the main road, wondering what was going on and where the Americans had come from. He had to drive for eight kilometres through the trees to get back to the main road, and on the way they suddenly found themselves surrounded by hundreds of tanks hidden among the palm groves on either side of the road. Some of them had their engines running. Mum started reciting parts of the Koran and praying to God to protect them while Dad drove as fast as he could, afraid that the bombing might start at any minute.

Mum, Dad and Uncle Ahmed were sweating and trembling with fear, but it wasn't over yet. When they finally got to the main road they found it jammed with people fleeing the capital, and they had to spend another hour and a half terrified, knowing that the Americans could bomb the road from their position on the bridge. The fighting had already started over there when they heard some huge explosions, which made them think the Iraqis must have blown up the bridge to stop the Americans crossing. So now we knew: Baghdad had been surrounded. From now on, the village where we were staying would be out of the way of the main fighting. But what about Baghdad itself? There were still millions of people there, and hundreds of thousands of soldiers. Would there be heavy fighting, or would the city surrender easily?

So much has happened today. Before sunset

we noticed that the track running past the village was full of cars and lorries – the main road that goes from Baghdad up to the north has been cut off by the Americans. So now people have to use the country track. We saw lots of soldiers who were running away from the fighting; one of them said their units had been completely wiped out, while others talked about the Americans' enormous firepower and their tanks, which can go as fast as normal cars.

In spite of all the upsetting things that have happened, there are still some funny things to laugh about. Dad was sitting indoors this afternoon watching two of our teenage cousins playing cards. He decided to tease them about a rumour that there are cars going around the villages rounding up boys to go and carry out attacks on the Americans – it was these rumours that were keeping them indoors.

'What are you two going to do if those gangs come round to take you to the front?' Dad asked them while they were playing cards. 'Why have you left the back door closed? I've already told you to leave it open just in case, so you can easily run away.' The boys quickly stopped playing cards and went to the back part of the house.

Suddenly there was a loud knock at the door. 'Looks like they've come to get you,' Dad said to them, and at that the two boys bolted out of the back door. As they ran off they saw two of our uncles with a group of other men swimming in the river. 'Run!' the boys said to them. 'They've come to take us to the front!' So the others took to their heels as well, while one of them went to tell his brothers, so that then there were even more of them running away to the fields. Just then a policeman on the nearby road was directing the traffic with a megaphone, but the men who were running away thought he was telling them to stop. They were all scared to bits – and all because of a knock at the door, which had just been a little girl looking for her mother! They only came back to the house once they'd been told what had really happened. They were so muddy. They'd climbed up trees and hidden in bushes. One man was wearing a new suit to visit his aunt when he heard the news and starting running. So instead of a beautiful suit he ended up with a very dirty one!

But there was truth in what my dad said. The Fedaeens are forcing people into the army and taking them to places where there is fighting. We don't want to lose the men in our families to the army. How would we women cope after that? Men in our country have the first word and the last word. And besides, most boys don't even know how to carry a gun let alone use one!

Monday, 7 April–Tuesday, 8 April 2003

Dear Diary,

Everywhere there are people camping out in the woods, just sleeping on small mattresses or sofa cushions. It is so sad to see them living without houses when they already have homes that they've run away from. I am so lucky to be staying in a house and sleeping in a proper bed. Lots of men from the village have given their houses over to the women and children, and have been sleeping in the fields themselves, while other people have been living in shops that are only half built.

Here in the village I have to dress differently when I go out. My whole body has to be covered and I have to walk in a way that is not natural to me. Usually I walk with my head held high, not like I'm hiding. But here I can't lift my eyes to somebody's face – I have to behave like someone who is shy or embarrassed. And I find it odd that women are expected to stay indoors looking after the children, rather than going out. This is a way of killing a woman's personality, but I have no choice, I have to do it.

We've got a big problem with water. Thank goodness my mum brought some from Baghdad. We have agreed that we must keep most of it for my sister Sama, because her stomach is so sensitive and she is so young. The rest of us can manage – we are all stronger and not so likely to get sick. Yes, kids should come first. Then after Sama, it should be Aula and then my mum and dad. My parents are getting older. I am a young woman, so I can cope.

We get the rest of our water from the river. We carry it in big bowls over our heads and fill up a very big tank. Usually Uncle Jasim's daughter, Florida, and I go to collect the water. We go backwards and forwards four or five times a day, so there is enough in the tank for everybody to wash dishes or use for our baths. And now we have to start drinking it, but first we boil it for at least ten minutes, let it cool and then boil it again.

Nobody here has fridges. They have freezers so they can freeze their food. There is only one fridge in the whole village, which we use to keep

Aula's insulin in. We have to walk ten minutes every morning and every evening so Aula can take her injection. But it is safer than keeping it cool down a well.

The end is coming for Baghdad. I just hope it's not going to be like watching a movie – a whole city full of dead people because of polluted air. Or maybe the buildings will explode and damage other buildings. It is very horrible to think about it. Like a nightmare, and I just wish this nightmare would finish quickly. But it's not. And it's not happening just at night anymore, it's happening during the day. Blood and death in Iraq: north, south, east and west. Killing: American, Iraqi and British. Men, women and children, everyone has his or her problems: food, water, safety, sleep and medicine. Everybody is tired. The question is always: *When will this war end?* And I ask myself: *What will happen next?*

Wednesday, 9 April 2003

Dear Diary,

Today's been a really exceptional day: the biggest statue of Saddam in Baghdad was pulled down.

It was painful to watch on TV – I had a kind of empty feeling inside, and tears in my eyes. I watched as an American soldier climbed up on top of the statue and wrapped the American flag round its head. No, I thought, it can't be true: Iraq an American colony. It was as if Baghdad itself had come to an end; as if everything that had gone before had finished and a new age was beginning. And what has the dawn of this new age brought? The Iraqis haven't got any say in anything any more. Where are the Iraqis, anyway? Where's Saddam's army, which was supposed to be so well trained? How could the Iraqis let all this happen? In the middle of Baghdad, as well – Baghdad, the capital of Iraq!

We were all looking at each other, unable to believe what was happening – it didn't seem possible that Saddam Hussein, with all his power, should be treated that way now that his rule has come to an end. I was sure he wouldn't have wanted it to finish like that. But now it was time for him to pay the price for everything he'd done in the past.

How can I explain all this to Sama, who used to have to say 'Long live our leader Saddam Hussein!' several times a day at school, and all the children would clap at the mention of his name? What am I going to tell her now? How can I make her go back to school when Saddam's reign is over and done with? But is he dead? No, he can't be. Sama won't understand, she'll still say, 'We love Saddam, we will sacrifice ourselves for him' – it's the result of a kind of brainwashing. But where is the sacrifice? Where's the loyalty to Saddam? It's all lies. It's as if we've been teaching our children make-believe things that don't really exist at all.

The end came on Wednesday 9 April 2003. I'll never forget it. It had a huge impact on the rest of the world too, like 11 September 2001 did, when the Twin Towers fell in New York. And just like the Americans will never forget that day, no Iraqi will ever forget 9 April, either. The strange thing is that there's a nine in both dates, which is one thing the Iraqis and the Americans have in common.

Thursday, 10 April 2003

Dear Diary,

Today the National Library was burnt and the National Museum destroyed. I could see how painful it was for Dad, he didn't know what to do. With so much sadness inside he was absorbed in his own thoughts. I know my father and I can read the expression in his eyes. I could see the pain there. Being a man he couldn't cry, but he was bottling it all up and he'd gone really pale. For him it means the loss of history – all those priceless manuscripts and books that so many people never had the chance to discover, and never will now. Now we have the spectacle of the doors of Saddam's palaces being deliberately flung open to let people in, even though they're still full of things. There's even been video footage showing what the palaces were like and how the bathrooms were all made of gold – everything beyond our wildest dreams. Unfortunately I wasn't able to see the whole programme, because I was busy doing other things like baking bread and milking the cow.

Eventually my uncle decided we should go back to Baghdad to make sure the house doesn't get burgled, because people have started looting Saddam's palaces and banks and government buildings.

We've all been wondering what orders have been given and asking anyone who comes to the village what's been going on in Baghdad, and how come the city has surrendered so quickly.

I couldn't hear the answers for myself, because I'm a girl and I'm not allowed to listen to those kind of conversations. But Dad told us what they said.

Apparently there's been fighting at Baghdad Airport and lots of people have been killed – some say there have been thousands of casualties. People have started talking about a strange kind of bomb that was used, but we don't know what it was. Whatever happened, the fighting was very heavy – as if all the fighting for Baghdad had been concentrated there in a single battle. The Information Minister says we're winning, by the grace of God. But no, we're not – we've lost, and it makes me sad just thinking about how my people are losing their homeland. Where are the people with any decency? Don't they exist?

Friday, 11 April 2003

Dear Diary,

People have begun looting the hospitals – the last places they should have thought of. What if one of the looters' relatives gets ill – where will they take them? Which hospital will they go to now? All the equipment's been stolen – patients in the wards have even been thrown on the floor so that the looters could take the beds! It breaks my heart just thinking about all the pain the patients must be going through, with no bed to sleep in, no way of sterilising anything, no surgical equipment for operations. What's got into the Iraqi people? Have they lost their minds? Just because Iraq has fallen, does that mean everything should be looted? These things already belong to all Iraqis as it is. But the looters won't get away with it: one day they'll all be punished for what they've done. How could they loot a place as important as a hospital that everyone needs? But even the doctors themselves have gone now, and people with injuries have no one to treat them.

Ordinary civilians have started helping each other now instead – I only wish I were there, so I could do something to help as well. But I can't – partly because I'm a girl, and partly because I haven't got enough experience. All I'd be able to do would be to try to make people feel a bit better by keeping them company and talking to them. But it makes me so unhappy that people would throw their fellow Iraqis, their brother Arabs and Muslims, on the floor just to steal their beds – and not even so they could sleep in them themselves, but in order to sell them! Some looters even stop ambulances in the street and loot everything inside. Everything's happening so quickly I can't take it all in; it's giving me a headache.

So much fear and pain. What's going to happen? Will we live or die? What's going to become of us? Is our house still standing, or has it been destroyed? Dad's worried. First of all he said that we should go back to Baghdad as soon as the fighting's over in Adhamiya. But later on we decided to go home tomorrow, and so we spent the evening packing. Granny was scared because Uncle Ahmed hasn't come back from the city yet, so Dad tried to calm her down. Baghdad may have fallen, but life goes on – we can't stay cooped up in the village forever.

There are nice things about village life, though. I've baked bread for the first time in my life; helped pick and wash oranges. I've also learnt how to milk a cow, even though normally its owner never allows anyone else to do it!

We've had some fun times and lots of laughs, despite everything that's been going on around us. It's just been a way of forgetting about all that. The funny thing is that I've become a real country bumpkin, which was one thing I wasn't expecting! It makes me laugh how my cousins spend the whole day out in the field where the chickens are kept, collecting eggs. In the evening we get together after supper and the young ones play all sorts of card games, sitting on the floor. From time to time the sitting-room windows rattle when an explosion goes off in the distance, but we usually carry on playing cards till about midnight, when the generators are turned off. Then it's time for us to go to bed, and only Dad and Jasim and As'ad stay up, sitting outside. As'ad is Mum's cousin, but he's only two years older than me so he's almost like a brother. Occasionally his mother, Auntie Basima, joins them too, if she can't sleep.

We talk about how the children spend their time enjoying themselves down by the river, and how us girls are going to tidy the house before the men get back. These are some of the happy things I'll remember about our time in the village, even though they've been anxious days as well. I'll never forget them.

Saturday, 12 April 2003

Dear Diary,

We left the village early this morning to go

home. But when we reached the outskirts of Baghdad we found rows and rows of people also making their way back to the city. Some would greet the Americans, and I remember that we saw the Americans pass the village, which was an indication that they were all over the whole country already.

There were a lot of burnt-out tanks by the road with their doors blown open and shrapnel lying about – the same tanks that we'd seen in good condition when we left Baghdad. We saw plenty of Americans close up. One was around my age. He had beautiful sunglasses, and when I got close I could see he was really handsome. I don't know why this soldier in particular caught my eye – it wasn't just the colour of his skin, it was something about him, his way of standing. I had all sorts of questions I wanted to ask him, to do with the way we saw him and the way he saw us. Will we and the Americans ever come to understand each another? Will I be able to talk to that soldier one day – that soldier, who's free to go wherever he likes in my country now? Are they more afraid of us than we are of them? And how will we ever be able to understand one another when they speak English and we speak Arabic? I tell Dad that if he comes near us, I hope he will be friendly – but I think he's probably a monster.

We all stayed silent till we got home. On the way we saw people walking hand-in-hand. There were women and children welcoming the Americans. From today onwards I don't think there will be any more fighting with missiles and tanks.

When we got home I went to open the garage door, and as soon as I'd unlocked it I saw Bambash jumping about all over the place, barking in a funny way and wagging his tail because he was so pleased we were back. I went over and picked him up and stroked him – I hadn't imagined till then that the dogs could miss us so much. I could see bullet marks on the walls of the house, perhaps because the Americans had tried to kill the dogs. But why would they do that? I know they love animals, so I don't think they'd want to kill them deliberately.

The house was dark. I went upstairs and opened my bedroom door. My room was a bit dusty but otherwise fine, and it was lovely to be back. I had a look round; the windows weren't broken, and everything else was just as I'd left it, too.

The looters had tried to steal the generator from the school next door to our house, but the neighbourhood vigilantes stopped them. We let them have Max for a while to help them protect the area. We're very proud of him, because he's such a brave dog. Then we cleaned part of the house, which had turned yellow from all the dust. We're back to the old routine of cleaning, eating, drinking and sleeping.

We had a light supper – just some bread and cheese. We were all tired, but I was happy because we were back in our own home with our own bathroom, though there's still a lot of work for us to do.

Sunday, 13 April 2003

Dear Diary,

This morning we carried on cleaning the house, and by lunchtime we'd put most of our things back in their usual places.

After lunch we decided to go and see Granny, Uncle Ahmed and my aunt. It was the first time I'd seen Baghdad in all the chaos – there's still looting going on all over the city. We headed downtown on the highway that runs through it from north to south, and the things we saw were horrifying. The Al-Nida'a Mosque, which is a big, impressive mosque that was finished a few months ago, was hit by tank fire during fighting between the Americans and the Iraqi militias. A lot of money had been spent on that building. Various colleges have been looted as well. From a distance we could see how several floors of the Iraqi Central Bank had been burnt out, and there was still smoke rising from many other government buildings.

We also saw lots of cars that had been damaged and stripped of all their parts, and there were big fuel tanks on both sides of the road with people taking as much as they wanted. There were still a lot of cars on the road loaded up with looted goods.

When we got to Granny's house we found everyone well. Uncle Ahmed described how there was hardly anyone else in the neighbourhood when he came back, but there was still fighting going on so he went out and bought a Kalashnikov and some ammunition for only four dollars. Later on some thieves broke into the schools opposite Granny's house and beat up the guard. When Uncle Ahmed saw what was going on he fired some shots in the air, which sent the thieves running.

After that we went to Jadiriya to see Uncle

Kadhim. Dad hadn't spoken to his brother for years because of a family rift. We were surprised to find him and his house completely unharmed.

On our way home we saw a lot of American soldiers patrolling the city. There were hardly any pedestrians in the streets and all the shops were closed.

Monday, 14 April 2003

Dear Diary,

We still don't have water or electricity, but we have food and our small generator.

I have my schoolbooks, but how can I go back to study? They showed my college on TV. It had been looted and everything we need to study, even the blackboard, has gone.

I see my life ahead of me as a long road. A long way until we get our lives back. My father says the Americans have created this chaos. I think this is part of the plan to destroy our country.

I wish I could be a doctor so I could do something to help people. Our city has only one hospital left open. So many people are wounded and need help.

I don't think my life will be normal, not soon. This year for me, my twentieth year, is already gone.

Tuesday, 15 April 2003

Dear Diary,

Today a BBC film crew came to film me because of my diary. Some of it has already appeared in *The Times* newspaper in the UK after I told a journalist I had met about it. Sama's started trying to learn a bit of English, so she could join in. While the rest of us were busy she went off to the playroom and came back a few minutes later with one of her drawings. It showed missiles and planes and soldiers and guns. We've done our best to put these images out of her mind, but the killed and injured children she saw on TV really made an impression on her. She's been full of questions, so somehow we've had to help her understand the new situation.

Mum got some food ready for our guests, which she was happy to do, even though she was exhausted by having to do so much work without electricity and while the water pressure is still very weak. She's watching how much cooking gas we have left very carefully, because if it runs out we'll have to use a paraffin stove instead. Without electricity the fridge won't work, so we can't keep anything in it.

Our guests loved Mum's cooking, which is far better than anything they can get in their hotels at the moment. What we wanted to show them was the kind of traditional Iraqi hospitality that was normal for us before the war. They didn't even notice that Mum and Dad didn't have anything to eat themselves.

In the evening our guests left, and we stayed up cleaning the house all over again – we've got to do it, because we're always expecting people to come round to see how we are. People go to see each other a lot at the moment during the day, because the phone lines are still down.

Thursday, 17 April–Saturday, 19 April 2003

Dear Diary,

These last few days have been some of the most special I've ever had, because I made a film about me and my life after part of my diary appeared in *The Times*. I had a great time. I made friends with two Americans and a South African in another TV crew, and they told me all about America, and the way of life there. They asked me all sorts of questions like what is life like now that the American soldiers are here, and what sort of difficulties we face. They also asked political questions, like what the Iraqi people feel about Saddam. It was all very new to me – no one's ever asked me these things before – but I answered them nevertheless.

In the end I was proud of what I'd done. All I wanted was for my voice to reach out to the world, so that maybe people will understand what's going on here and what the Iraqi people are going through – even if I'm not an expert.

Monday, 21 April 2003

Dear Diary,

I woke up early today to go and see my new friends at the Palestine Hotel, where all the journalists stay. On the way I talked to an American soldier for the first time. He had bright blue eyes and I could tell he felt proud, sitting on top of his tank. I asked him why he was wearing a flak jacket, when the weather was so hot and no one was going to shoot at him now anyway. He told me it was a safety measure, in case someone shot at him from a distance. He seemed to be making fun of me, and his friends were laughing at him because he hadn't been expecting to meet an Iraqi girl who could speak English. There were other tanks nearby and they looked frightening – some of them had things like cowboys and skulls painted on them. One of them had its door open and I could see all the equipment inside. I don't understand how soldiers can live inside a big heap of metal like that!

I also met another soldier, and it was the first time he'd met an Iraqi girl who could speak English as well. I let him have his picture taken with me so that he could show it to his family. All the soldiers were young and sweltering in the heat. People said they were only there to make some money and then go back to their country. If that's true, it's tragic that people fight for money. They're from all sorts of races. Some of them are friendly, but others are nervous.

The hotel was full of journalists all working in radio and television. The American TV crew told me that it had been even more packed when the statue of Saddam was pulled down.

The journalists have soldiers especially to protect them, as well as doctors looking after them and interpreters translating for them. I felt sorry for them because they all seemed so tired and yet unable to relax. If was as if they were going through some of the same difficulties as the rest of us. They can't get water or food easily either, so I can sympathize with them. I'd like to go back there another time.

Tuesday, 22 April 2003

Dear Diary,

During the last few days tens of thousands of people of all ages have been walking in small groups to the holy city of Najaf. Tomorrow it'll be forty days since the anniversary of the death of the Prophet Muhammad's grandson Hussein, in a battle hundreds of years ago. Hussein is a very important person for the Shiites. Some of the people going to join in the ceremonies tomorrow will walk up to eighty kilometres to get there. He's actually buried in Kerbala, where he was killed, but the ceremonies always happen in Najaf, which is where his father Ali's tomb is.

This year the ceremonies are bound to be

different now that the Shiites are rid of Saddam, who used to stop them from practising their traditions. And there'll also be several of the Shiite political leaders there who've returned from Iran during the last few days, after more than twenty-five years in exile.

Wednesday, 23 April 2003

Dear Diary,

Today we all visited our friend Qusay, who's known Dad since they were both young men. His wife is a beautiful woman called Aida and, for the first few years of their marriage they didn't have any children so ended up adopting their first son, Ali.

A few years later, Aida had a baby boy of her own who they called Fahad, and after that another boy called Salam, but that didn't stop them loving Ali. Ever since I was little we've always played together and been very fond of each other.

Now everything in Qusay's family has changed because of the war. On 3 April there was bombing in Doura where they live. Fahad, who was sixteen years old, was indoors when he heard people in the street calling for help; lots of soldiers and civilians had been badly wounded by cluster bombs. Fahad couldn't help himself and rushed outside to see what he could do, even though his father had told him not to leave the house. He managed to save two people and help them get to hospital, but soon afterwards he was wounded himself when another cluster bomb went off.

The doctors did everything they could, but they weren't able to save him and he died the next day. He was one of almost thirty people in his area killed in the bombing. He's left us forever now, but I'm proud of how brave he was in giving his own life to save other people he didn't even know.

The family were all dressed in black. It was very difficult for us to go into their home knowing that we wouldn't see our childhood friend again. I've never been through anything like this before. Qusay was sitting reading the Koran. He was composed as he greeted us, but Dad was crying. Soon afterwards Aida left the room saying, 'My son proved how brave he was, before those bastards' bombs killed him.' She was in floods of tears, and the rest of us were all crying by then as well. There was a big picture of Fahad on the wall, surrounded by passages from the Koran. We see Fahad as a martyr because he was a peaceful person who died while trying to help others. We listened to the story of what he had done and how he had spent his last moments in his father's arms.

Thursday, 24 April–Friday, 25 April 2003

Dear Diary,

The time goes by so slowly and everything's so monotonous. In the morning we clean the house and get the food ready, then we have a little nap in the afternoon and after that we have people over and chat.

We found out that one of my cousins lost his best friend during the war. He had tears in his eyes when he told me, and we were both going through the same feelings. I said to him, 'You know, I lost a friend too, God rest his soul.'

I was really sad when the TV crew left. They're the first American friends I've ever had and I felt as though I'd lost them.

On the radio they keep playing the same old songs over and over – it's so boring. I've tried to tune into other stations, but I can't find any. The only way I know what's happening on the streets is through Dad's friends, because we aren't allowed to go out. The Iraqi people don't know the meaning of the words 'democracy' and 'freedom'. To them, 'freedom' means being able to do whatever they want and break the law and even kill people – a freedom from religion and tradition. But none of that means they're free in the true sense. The only way people can be happy is by supporting one another. My people are destroying the meaning of the word 'freedom'.

Saturday, 26 April 2003

Dear Diary,

Today I saw a mass grave for the first time on TV. It was in Mosul, and it was a horrific sight – there were the remains of bodies lying on top of each other, and people were putting them in bags and removing them so they could be identified. There were so many of them, it was very sad to see.

I've also heard that we're going to be going back to school and college, although Mum's afraid of us getting kidnapped, which has been happening to more and more girls lately. It's a terrifying thought.

There is a lot of crime these days. In some ways, if the Baath Party were still around, it would be safer because they'd keep things under control. The Baath Party is the political party that has ruled Iraq since 1968, until this war started. Like so many families in Iraq, mine used to work for the party – well, not me and Mum and my sisters, but Dad did. And the party was not all bad. They did solve all sorts of problems, but the Americans don't make distinctions.

There are always good and bad people wherever you go – no two people are alike, just like no two fingers of a hand are the same. And that applies to the American troops as well: there are some who like to do their best for people and who don't like waving guns in Iraqi people's faces, but who have to obey orders, and then there are bad-natured ones who are out to hurt people and get revenge.

My country's going through the worst of times now, but some of us are sticking together. In my neighbourhood we all help each other, doing things like contributing to the gas we need to power the generator, so that we can try to keep an electricity supply going.

We can't take the car out, so we walk to the market to buy food. We don't get much, because we can't keep anything cold. The electricity supply isn't reliable enough to power the fridge, and we've been without electricity for two weeks now. We took Aula's insulin to Dad's friend's house again, to keep it cold. When the electricity supply came on today, we all jumped for joy. It's given us hope that it might come back on more regularly.

Will my country ever be at peace? I ask myself. The problem now isn't just the Americans, it's the Iraqis themselves, who've started killing each other. It's terrible. We've been told not to go near anything lying on the ground if we can't tell what it is, in case it's a bomb. That made us realize the streets really aren't safe at the moment. I've learnt a lot this year and gained a lot, but what do the years ahead hold in store for me?

Monday, 28 April 2003

Dear Diary,

Today is Saddam's 66th birthday. There used to be big celebrations for a week either side of the day itself, with street parties and people chanting Saddam's name. Saddam himself used to celebrate his birthday in his hometown, Tikrit, and children from all parts of the country used to go there specially. Watching TV on that day was always dead boring, because all they'd show from ten o'clock in the morning all the way through till night-time, were things like people singing nationalistic songs praising Saddam.

This year there haven't been any celebrations, because Saddam's disappeared. But I heard that there have been some celebrations in Tikrit all the same, and people say the Americans joined in and that there were journalists reporting on it and everyone drinking champagne. Maybe it's because the people of Tikrit are still under Saddam's influence, but it seemed funny that the Americans would join in the festivities, when they were the ones who pulled his statue down. Maybe they wanted to wish him an *unhappy* birthday, now that he's lost the war and his power?

Sometimes I think, *Why can't I go out?* Just because I'm a girl and girls have to stay indoors and their opinions don't count – it's men who are always in charge of everything. But I'll keep writing my diary, and maybe one day it will be published. For me it would be enough if only one person read it.

Wednesday, 30 April 2003

Dear Diary,

Up until today there's been a curfew, which means we can't go out between eleven o'clock at night and six o'clock in the morning, but it's now been changed to four o'clock in the morning, because that's when the dawn prayers are held in the mosques. But the streets are still deserted after sunset anyway. Everyone's afraid of thieves and other criminals. We've become like chickens, going to bed early and getting up early. Life is so boring at the moment. We've got money problems and trouble getting petrol for the car, too. It's become so expensive and so hard to find – you have to queue for ages at petrol stations. Some people fill up their cars and then siphon out the petrol later and sell it on the black market. Why would they do that? Our country is an oil producer! None of these things used to happen before the war.

The American Defence Secretary Donald Rumsfeld has come to Iraq, which is important, because he's such a powerful figure in the US government. There's been talk about how the Americans are in control of Iraq's oil, and how a pipeline's going to be built between Kirkuk in northern Iraq, and Israel. Almost all the Iraqi people hate the Israelis because they kill Palestinians and it seems, don't want to make peace with them. Is the situation between the Iraqis and the Americans going to end up like that? Saddam used to say that Iraq and Palestine were one and the same cause. I hope they find a solution, because so many people have been killed already and I want there to be peace in the world.

Thursday, 1 May 2003

Dear Diary,

Today is International Labour Day. Normally it would be a public holiday and we'd be able to sleep in, and then, instead of doing our homework, we could go out and enjoy ourselves. But this year we couldn't, because of all the things that are going on in the streets. Women who don't wear their headscarves are being kidnapped by men who think that their behaviour is disrespectful to our religion. It's much safer to wear a headscarf; that way you don't draw any unwanted attention to yourself. People are having their cars stolen, and there are even children carrying weapons and fooling around with them, as if they were acting out an Arnold Schwarzenegger or Jean-Claude van Damme film. There are ten and twelve-year-olds wandering about with machine guns, and the only thing that stops them is if an American comes along and takes their weapons away. People are afraid of each other. The Americans are trying to disarm people, but the Iraqis are too clever for them and hide their weapons in order to defend themselves if they're attacked. In Saddam's time people stuck up for each other more, and all a girl had to do was scream for people to come running to the rescue. So why do people behave any differently now?

The Shiite demonstrators in Paradise Square are crazy – they stand around in circles lashing themselves. Is it because Saddam banned them from doing that, so that now they want to do it even more? Some of them even beat themselves on the back with metal chains until they bleed, but others just slap themselves with their bare hands. I support the way Saddam banned practices like those, because I think they're shameful. But everyone's free to do as they choose, I suppose. As for me, my freedom doesn't extend beyond the walls of our house, since I still can't go out because Mum and Dad are afraid for my safety. Mum got even more worried when Sama said she wanted to go back to school – she's determined that none of us should go back yet.

One of our neighbours is a taxi driver and goes to petrol stations from time to time. He told me that some of the Americans there have started using Iraqi slang words, like '*ishteh*', which means 'move it!' – except they pronounce them in a funny way. Could this be a sign of a new understanding between the Iraqis and the Americans?

Today we heard some gun shots, and later on we were told that people had been firing their guns to celebrate the fact that the electricity supply had been turned back on for a couple of hours in their area. We're always hearing shots being fired all over the place – it makes us afraid that stray bullets might hit us, so usually we stay inside. Firing guns like that seems to me a primitive way of celebrating.

These days people are selling DVDs with

pornographic films on them, which used to be banned. We've heard people are selling pornographic magazines, too. Why are people turning so bad? We have our traditions and most Iraqis are Muslims; have we really changed so much? I suppose it's because these things used to be forbidden, but personally I'd rather read a good book than see one of those films. Maybe I'm a bit of a prude, but I've been brought up by a mother and father who've taught me the difference between right and wrong, and we'd be embarrassed just to hear the word 'sex'.

My sisters have started thinking about returning to school, but they're still too scared to go back just yet. I'm terrified of losing either of them too, but we don't want them to miss the rest of the school year, and they don't want to go back later than their friends. So we've finally decided that they can go, and we've started getting everything ready – cleaning their satchels and getting their pens organized. As for me, I still don't know when I'm going back to college. Now there will be both male and female students there, and I don't know what sort of problems I might have. I hope the boys don't try to control us.

Saturday, 3 May 2003

Dear Diary,

Today the schools did reopen as planned, but Mum and Dad decided not to send Aula and Sama back until they can make sure it's safe enough. All the same, the girls who go to the middle school next to our house were all really pleased to be back. They all live in the neighbourhood so they weren't in any danger, because people who aren't from around here don't dare come into the area – the criminals know they're not the only ones with guns. All the girls were wearing their dark-blue uniforms and white blouses. There weren't any classes today because some of the teachers hadn't been able to make it, so instead the girls cleaned up the building. The school management has offered to pay the teachers $20 per month for the time being.

In the afternoon I went out shopping near the house with the rest of my family. The market mostly had dried foods, but we managed to find some bread and vegetables, and a big chicken that we took home to cook. Dad drove very fast, because of the risk of someone trying to steal the car, but we had to go out to get the essentials.

On the way I saw an American talking to a

little boy; the boy didn't speak English and the American didn't speak Arabic, so they were communicating with gestures. The boy wanted the American to give him some drinking water, but the soldier didn't understand and in the end gave him some sweets and shook his hand. The boy went away happy all the same. I also saw old people sitting in cafés drinking tea and coffee and playing backgammon and dominoes.

Today I saw girls going to the school in our neighbourhood wearing their lovely uniforms and accompanied by their parents, because they're afraid for them. But the school was full today.

I've heard that I'll be able to go back to college on Friday. I'm so happy, because I'll get to see my friends – but I'm worried about finding out that I've lost any of them, too. Just thinking that I'm going back at last has really cheered me up, and I've already got all my books together.

Sunday, 4 May 2003

Dear Diary,

Over the last few days, while Sama's been getting ready to go back to school, I've been teaching her some maths – just simple things like basic sums. Mum's given her some lessons in writing Arabic, too. She's overjoyed to be going back, because she hasn't been able to play with her friends for such a long time. Aula doesn't want to wear a headscarf, which is a problem. I've told her she'll be safer wearing it, to avoid attracting people's attention.

All the same, we do want freedom for women – they shouldn't have to just stay at home. But we haven't got any choice – a man's opinion always counts for more than a woman's. In my country there's no such thing as women's liberation – even though women make up half of society.

Aula told me how the family of one of her friends had lost their house, and had nothing left but the clothes they were wearing. *What would we do if something like that happened to us?* I asked myself.

Monday, 5 May 2003

Dear Diary,

Things are becoming unbearable. Life has no meaning any more. There's no work for people to earn a living. Dad's unemployed, but there's nothing I can do except help Mum with the housework. The situation is too much for me – the only way I can escape from it all is by sleeping for hours on end. The music they play on the coalition radio station is hardly what I feel like listening to at the moment – how can we be cheerful, when the chaos is getting worse by the day? Instead of giving us any encouraging news, the people on the radio just tell us to cooperate more. We still haven't got a regular power supply, and most of the time the electricity is cut off. Sama plays on the computer and watches her favourite Disney films when we have power, but the family can't buy a satellite dish because it would eat into our savings, which are running out fast enough as it is.

In the midst of all the chaos, some people are taking advantage of the lack of government controls to flood the market with satellite dishes. People are keen to buy them even though they don't really know enough about them. There have also been thousands of cars imported from neighbouring Arab countries. Before, if anyone wanted to buy an imported car they had to pay all kinds of taxes, although in recent years the government let people buy imported cars for work, like lorries and pick-up trucks. But now you see all sorts of cars in the streets without number plates, and there's nothing anyone can do about it. People like Dad who own properly registered cars have started taking off the number plates and putting them inside their cars, because otherwise the plates might get stolen.

Wednesday, 7 May 2003

Dear Diary,

I woke up at nine o'clock this morning to hear American helicopters flying over the house. I looked out of my bedroom window; it was the first time I'd seen them flying so low.

I've started revising to get ready to go back to college. There's still no electricity, so even though it's incredibly hot I can't turn on the air conditioning or even the lights. It's impossible to keep my spirits up or do anything for fun. The family's been arguing too. Everyone's having a bad time in their own way. Sama hasn't got anyone to play with, and the visits we used to make to our friends and relatives have all come to an end.

This morning I stood outside the house and watched people go by. I saw the girls from the local middle school going home at 11.30 a.m., even though they normally finish at 2.30 p.m. One of them told me it's because they only have three lessons a day at the moment instead of seven, like they used to. All the same, it's still a good sign that they're determined to finish the year at all, no matter what.

I'm going back to college on 17 May until the beginning of July, which is when the end-of-year exams start. I don't know what it'll be like.

This evening I went out for a walk with Dad, in the park near our house where the kings of Iraq are buried. It was the first time I'd been out after dark since the war ended. We'd all decided to have kebabs for supper, so Dad and I went to the local kebab restaurant, which only reopened yesterday, to get them. I saw some young boys driving along playing really loud music in their car. People drive around so fast it's crazy – but there's no one to stop them.

Friday, 9 May 2003

Dear Diary,

All Adhamiya is getting ready to celebrate the Prophet Muhammad's birthday, which is one of our most important religious festivals. Everyone in the district gets together to put up decorations in all the neighbourhoods around the place where Abu Hanifa's buried; he was a very important religious person during the Middle Ages. His tomb was hit by artillery fire during the fighting, and it'll cost a fortune to restore it.

It looks as though this year's festivities will be special, given the situation the country's in, and some people think the traditional get-together by Abu Hanifa's tomb is going to be more political than religious. There are still American army vehicles parked at the entrance to the mosque, which infuriates the people who go to pray there. In recent years thousands of people have always gone to the mosque for the evening celebrations, especially women and children, and there are candles everywhere lighting up the place and lots of food given to the poor. But this year the festivities are being held during the daytime, because of the lack of electricity and security. Every year I used to go to the mosque and pray and light candles – it was lovely. This year is the first year that I won't celebrate the Prophet's birthday, because the men in our neighbourhood have decided that Muslim women should not be able to celebrate. Local women and children have been warned not to go in case things turn nasty. It's a special day for me, so I feel very upset.

Saturday, 10 May 2003

Dear Diary,

Today Aula had an argument with Mum about having to wear a headscarf and baggy clothes to cover herself up and avoid attracting people's attention. Sama was really happy to be going back to school, and I helped Mum get all her books and things ready. Aula is getting ready too.

When they got to school, instead of starting lessons straight away all the girls went round seeing how everyone was. Aula has told me all sorts of stories she heard from the others, like how lots of girls have had their homes destroyed or burnt down, and how loads of them left Baghdad during the fighting and went to the countryside, just like we did. Lots of things are missing from the school and all the desks and chairs have been smashed up. But what gave us the biggest fright was when Aula said they hadn't been allowed to go into their classroom because there was a dead body in there. Who could have done all that – and why? Luckily most of the school records are still intact, but some of them have been burnt, including the ones with all the girls' exam results. Apparently the English teacher asked the girls all kinds of questions, but I don't know how much that'll have helped.

As for me, I've spent the day helping Mum clean the house – every day so much dust comes indoors! The electricity and water are still cut off, and who knows when they'll come back on again.

Mum was really worried about the girls today, which is only natural. Dad brought them home at lunchtime in a taxi. Sama was really excited to have seen her friends again; she's been told that the school's going to stay open and her teachers have given her some reading and maths homework to do. Aula said that most of the other girls were wearing headscarves, but according to Sama they don't have to wear school uniforms any more.

Sunday, 11 May 2003

Dear Diary,

We all wear headscarves whenever we go out now. At Aula's school religious men have started hanging posters on the wall saying that all girls have to wear them. It's even reached the point where little girls are wearing them: Sama says she wants one, because all her friends have got them. They act as a kind of protection. None of us put on any make-up either, to avoid attracting unwanted attention. There are even people in the street who try to pressure women and girls into covering their hair. Women who go out uncovered are in danger of been attacked. I find all of this very upsetting. Why should men control what a women wears?

Monday, 12 May 2003

Dear Diary,

Today's the Prophet Muhammad's birthday. Granny came over to see us, and we talked about everything that's been going on lately and about how we used to celebrate this day in the past. We used to go down to have dinner near the river, and then we'd go to the celebrations in the Abu Hanifa Mosque. But this year we couldn't go, partly because it was too dangerous and partly because women weren't allowed to go out in Adhamiya. Some people had walked there from Kadhmiya, and the whole area was so packed that eventually some of the roads were closed off. Traditionally people light candles on the Prophet's birthday and go and visit their relatives, but this year all that's been banned by the men of the neighbourhood, which really upset me.

All the same, our friend Jihan came round to have tea and cake with us. She's a reporter, and she was wearing a headscarf for the first time in her life. When she saw herself in the mirror she thought she looked funny, but we told her it was a good idea to wear it, as a precaution.

Wednesday, 14 May 2003

Dear Diary,

Today I went to the BBC's office to take a test, to see if I could get a job there as a reporter. At least it would be better than sitting at home all day, especially when I'm not sure whether the colleges are really going to reopen soon. If I become a journalist I'll be able to write reports and earn some money to help my family – and anyway, writing is already one of my hobbies: that's why I've been writing this diary. I've always dreamt of becoming a doctor and of writing reports at the same time about things that people like hearing about, and which need to be described.

On my way to the building where the BBC staff work I saw some British soldiers. They have a particular way of marching and taking orders; we could tell the difference between them and the Americans. The British are in charge of southern Iraq at the moment.

There are only a few more days left to go before I'm supposed to be going back to college, but with the way things are at the moment I've got a feeling that I'll have to stay at home.

Thursday, 15 May 2003

Dear Diary,

This morning I helped clean the house, especially with all the visitors we've had. We like to have our Persian carpet out all year round, although it gets so hot in summer that most other families take their carpets up at this time of year and then put them back down in November when winter starts approaching.

While I was doing the cleaning I fell and cut my toe on a piece of glass. It really hurt and running it under cold water didn't help. It was bleeding a lot, and I couldn't help crying because it hurt so much. I couldn't put my shoe on and I was worried because I'm supposed to be going back to college soon, so I decided to go to the hospital. But when I got there, there was no one who could see me, and not even any disinfectant, so I had to go and get some from a chemist myself, as well as some bandages. It made me think of all the people who've died because there's no one to treat them in the hospitals – not even any nurses – and then I thought about how my friend Fahad had died. I was so depressed after this that I couldn't help Mum with the housework today.

Friday, 16 May 2003

Dear Diary,

My toe hurt so much I couldn't sleep properly all last night. This afternoon I finished preparing to go back to college tomorrow, and got my clothes and all my books ready.

Saturday, 17 May 2003

Dear Diary,

This morning I woke up early. My parents had been agonizing for days over whether or not I should go back to college, but in the end there was no other option. All the students at my college have to pay fees, and Mum and Dad have sacrificed a lot to pay for me to go there. For a girl like me, studying at a place like that will give me a much more secure future. Being a chemist is seen as a respectable job for women in my country, and lots of women prefer to go to chemists run by other women too. And as well as all that, girls who've been to the College of Pharmacology have better chances of making a good marriage.

Mum and Dad didn't want me to have to repeat another year, and they both think things are bound to get better as time goes by. And the route I take to college has American troops all along it, so there aren't many criminals about.

This morning Dad took my sisters to school

first, and then it was my turn. On my way to college I gradually started feeling more hopeful and less scared, although I was still a bit worried about what might happen. We saw lots of other families taking their children to the various colleges in the centre of the city, including plenty of girls. Everything looked encouraging.

As soon as the taxi driver dropped us off at Baghdad Medical City, I could see all the damage that had been done to the different buildings. What upset me most wasn't the fact that the gardens had all dried up. It was what the Americans based there with their tanks and their armoured personnel carriers had done to the place. They'd taken over the big conference centre for themselves, and since the whole area was completely open, with no walls separating the different parts, they'd piled dozens of cars on top of each other to build a kind of defensive barrier for themselves. Apart from the waste of using brand-new cars like that, what really struck me was how they didn't take any care of the place, either. I suppose that's war for you.

I couldn't help wondering what else I was going to see after that, and whether any of the other students or our professors had been killed. The first thing I noticed about my college building itself was that all the entrances were clean, which was a good sign – at least it meant that someone had been looking after it. I saw some of my classmates outside, who were all pleased to see me and said how relieved they were that I was all right. The ones who didn't turn up today are waiting for us to let them know how things are. Everyone's nervous about coming to college because the roads are so dangerous and there's so little petrol.

Once we went inside the college we went to greet our professors. Dad wanted to find out what the new college timetable would be. The assistant dean told us the college would be open five days a week, from nine o'clock in the morning till one o'clock in the afternoon. The gates of the college will be kept tightly closed while we're studying, to prevent any strangers from coming in, and our parents can help guard the college if they want to.

I walked around the college and saw that the same sorts of things had been stolen from here as from my sisters' schools. Inside the buildings the doors had all been smashed up, as had a lot of the furniture. But the classrooms were mostly all right, and we'll be able to use them. We'll just have to get used to the heat for the last few weeks of term, now that the air-conditioning units have been taken.

There was a lot of heated discussion going on inside the college about what we should change its name to. It used to be called the Leader's College of Pharmacology: the 'leader' being Saddam Hussein. Everyone soon settled on calling it the Baghdad College of Pharmacology.

On the way home I saw masses of graffiti on walls everywhere. Some of it was anti-Saddam, but a lot of it was calling on people to join the dozens of different political parties that have sprung up now. Every group or party says it's the best equipped to decide Iraq's future. There are American troops in all the big squares and at the junctions of all the main roads in the city.

Going back to college today has given me some hope for the future. All my classmates were fine, and even though lots of students' homes had got damaged in the war, none of it was too serious. Some of the students are still abroad in places like Syria and Jordan, but on their way back to Iraq now. We'd all been so worried about each other. Diary, I can't express how happy I am that my friends are alive and well. We're all scared about the future but things will get better – it's just a matter of time.

Sunday, 18 May–Saturday, 31 May 2003

Dear Diary,

I'm not writing so regularly now. I'm busy trying to catch up at college and life is returning, more or less, to normal. At any rate, the war itself and the really hard times are over, I think, and everything is in control of the Americans.

Despite the shortened class schedule, Aula has done well at school and she's been moved up to the next grade. Luckily we managed to get hold of enough insulin before the war started to last several months, but the needles she needs for her injections cost three times more than they used to. She's always going on at Dad about how we should all leave Iraq and go to England, which is where she was born, and she says Dad should apply for her to get a British passport. She worries about Dad and always kisses him whenever he goes out or comes home. She spends all day cooped up in the house, which has become a kind of prison for all of us. Mum and Dad are thinking about sending her on a kind of study course during the summer holidays with some other girls who live nearby, to keep her occupied. They've discussed it with one of our neighbours, a teacher who's offered to tutor the girls, but he's asking for quite a lot of money in return.

Sunday, 1 June 2003–Tuesday, 3 June 2003

Dear Diary,

In a few weeks the term will be over at college and I'll be back at home again. Our exams should be normal, but they have spread them out more so we have a chance to go back and review what we had studied before the war.

Some people don't want women to be allowed to study – they're religious people known as Wahhabis, and it didn't come as a big surprise that they would demand that male and female students be taught separately. Anyway, I stick to my family's advice and stay out of all those arguments. All I want is to be a good student and achieve my dreams.

Baghdad has been completely swamped with new things: satellite dishes and satellite phones and all kinds of food. You can find everything under the sun here, even drugs and pornographic films. But everything's so expensive. People say the Americans aren't doing enough to make the city safe, and no one dares go out after dark.

When evening comes, the place is like a ghost town.

We don't have very much contact with other people at the moment, because no one can go out and only the men are able to go and see how their friends and relations are doing. Sama is always crying because she's not allowed to leave the house; she spends most of her time playing with her Barbie dolls, drawing and watching cartoons.

Wednesday, 4 June 2003

Dear Diary,

Today's my birthday. I'm twenty now and I celebrated with a few friends at college. But because things are still difficult we just had some cake and fizzy drinks, nothing expensive.

Though I am no longer a teenager, I still feel there is a lot to learn in life. But I still have the same silly sense of humour that I've had since I was a kid! When will I grow up? I wonder – I hope people will start to see me as an adult now.

Final entry (undated)

Dear Diary,

I leave my story in your safekeeping – the story of an Iraqi girl who hasn't discovered much about life yet; a girl who already had missiles exploding all around her when she was in her mother's womb; a girl who has lived through war and fear and cruel sanctions on her country; a girl whose parents are always worried; a girl whose little sisters are terrified by the bombs and the looters, and come to her for comfort; a girl with American soldiers all around her neighbourhood, every bit as scared as she is; a girl born in the wrong place at the wrong time – but a girl who still has hope.

I'll get myself to America one day – not to take revenge, but to study and live and love like anyone else. No matter how many missiles President Bush rains down on me or how many soldiers he sends to my country, nothing is going to stop me. And once I'm there, I'll go and see the families of American soldiers killed in Iraq and those who are still fighting too, to offer them my condolences.

I'll do the same thing in Britain as well. I'm going to go to Hyde Park and go for walks in

Oxford to collect chestnuts, just like I used to when I was little. And I'll go and see my teacher at my old school, Upper Red Land, which I've never forgotten, and I'll visit the families of soldiers sent by Tony Blair to fight in the deserts of Iraq. I'll tell them the same thing that I said to Iraqi families who have lost sons and yet still cling on to life: *The future is shining in front of us like a bright light, and eventually we'll find that we can all live together as long as there's no darkness and no injustice between us. While there's still light, no one will be able to destroy our lives completely.*

I have to go now. It's time for me to write another diary about different things, not to be published, but for me to leave to my children one day. Goodbye, Diary.

Afterword

I hoped things would get better after the war was over. In time we were able to go out and visit other families who lived near us. The weather was really hot, which was awful, and everyone was upset because we still didn't have regular electricity and water and the telephones were still cut off. But this was when Dad got us a new satellite dish, and after that at least we were able to find out what was going on in the rest of the world. It made us realize why Saddam had banned satellite television, to try and cut us off from outside news.

Dad decided not to go back to work any more, because the situation was so bad and someone might even have tried to kill him, now that there was a witch-hunt for former Baathists going on. There was much crime and many kidnapping attempts in Baghdad. But despite all these problems, many of our friends continued to come and see us.

On Tuesday 22 July, Saddam's sons Uday and Qusay were killed. At first we didn't believe it, but then we saw their bodies on TV. After that we were glad they'd been killed, because of the brutal way they'd always treated people and all the harm they'd done. I think most Iraqis felt the same way. I guess Saddam, too, came to understand what it means to lose a son.

After I was filmed talking about my diary in the spring, some of the journalists I knew started to think it might be possible for me to study in the United States. It's such an exciting opportunity for me, because that country is full of people from all over the world, with all sorts of religions and cultures and ways of thinking. Before long, I got news that one of America's best universities, the University of Pennsylvania, was interested in my story. After phone calls, faxes and e-mails with them, I got a letter that changed my life.

It was from Mr Lee Stetson, the dean of admissions at the university. He offered me a chance to come to school in Philadelphia. The university also offered to fully fund my four years there, with financial aid grants.

Everything happened so fast and different members of my family had different opinions. Some of them were in favour of me going, and others were against it. But in the end my father decided that I should go. I was glad because I was going to a world that was completely new to me, but also sad, because I would be leaving my family behind. I was worried about them because the situation in Baghdad was still so dangerous. But they were very understanding, and they knew it was the right thing for me to do. We knew that in any case, we'd all stay in touch and always care about each other.

When the time came for me to leave the house I read part of the Koran, and then said goodbye to everyone. We had tears in our eyes. I think the hardest thing for my family was to let me travel on my own and live on my own resources. Where I'm from, a girl wouldn't normally be allowed so much freedom, and that's why some members of my family didn't agree with me going. That's also why I left for America secretly. Only certain people knew that I was going, and I didn't even say goodbye to all of them. Despite the objections of Granny and my uncles, my parents were proud of me and told me to study hard.

I left Baghdad on Tuesday 26 August and went with an escort to the airport. Along the way, I listened to the orders the American soldiers were being given. They were about what to do in case they were attacked. It seemed to me that they were brave to have left their families to come and do their duty in Iraq. They all seemed homesick and even had photos of their families with them. But to me, it looked as if the soldiers considered each other like a family. Finally we got to the airport. I thanked them and then set off for America.

Since arriving in Philadelphia in August, I have learned many things – both inside and outside of my classes. America is a place where there are all kinds of possibilities and a real understanding of the concept of freedom.

I could never give enough thanks to Dean Stetson, the University of Pennsylvania and everyone else who helped me to experience these things. One day, I hope to help the university make another student's dream come true.

As I work to succeed at college, I'm always being asked how I feel about what is still going on in Iraq. It is difficult to know from the news, but I'm worried about my family. They're facing the danger of being kidnapped or robbed – or just living life after the war.

I hope there aren't any more confrontations with the Americans and that the two sides can come to understand each other. That is the reason I wrote this diary. I wanted to try to bring about a greater understanding of my country and to show what Iraqis are really like. I wanted people to know what it's like for children to have no hope. I wanted them to know what it means for a father to work for hours just to feed his family. I wanted them to know what it is like to have to flee from home.

I wanted to make the Americans and the British understand that we are not their enemies. We just need some security and the chance to lead normal lives. Let's give the children the opportunity to be happy; let's give people the chance to live and hope, to help others, and bring an end to all their suffering.

I believe that there is a book in every person's life, and every book must have an ending. I hope the day comes when I can read my diaries to my children, and they can learn from my experiences to avoid making the same mistakes I made. And I hope, one day, to help Iraq and the rest of the world walk together towards peace and happiness.

Postscript

14 December 2003

Dear Diary,

Today is a historic day. It's been confirmed that Saddam Hussein was captured last night. The Americans have been searching for him for more than eight months, since the day that his statue fell. Now that the most powerful member of the regime is gone, I feel that his story and his history are finished too. It is hard to believe.

I got the news after a long night of studying for my final exams at college. It was 5:30 a.m., and I was sleeping, when I heard the sound of an incoming e-mail message on my computer. I thought it was probably from someone in my family, but I was so exhausted that I did not get out of bed for another hour and a half. When I opened the e-mail, I thought it was a joke.

My mother was writing to tell me about the capture and that there was gunfire in the air all over Baghdad in celebration. She said my dad was picking Aula and Sama up from school and she was worried about stray bullets hitting one of them. But then she said that they all arrived home safely and the family gathered around the TV to watch the news.

When I read my mom's message, I couldn't believe my eyes. I remembered a few days earlier, when my dad told me he had heard that Saddam's associate, Azat Al-Dury had been captured, and it turned out not to be true. So in this case, I wanted to play it safe. I wrote back to my family and said I hoped Dad would be careful. Like all Iraqi families, mine was having a hard time with life after the war. If Dad got injured now, they would have even more difficulty – and I would not be there to help.

That thought made me nervous, so I started to look for the news on the Internet. When I found out that Saddam really had been caught, I was shocked. I'd thought Saddam might disappear like Osama Bin Laden had done. But as I read the news, it started to make more sense to me. I had always thought that if Saddam was captured, it would probably be in Tikrit, where he was born. But I never thought he would be found in a hole in the ground!

It reminded me of a story that came out after the war, about a man who hid for many years inside the wall of his house. In that story, the man was hiding from Saddam's regime. And now, this time, it is Saddam himself who has had to hide in the same way from all the people who were looking for him.

I was so excited, I wanted to see more. My housemate has a TV, but she was still asleep when I got the news. I had a hard time waiting for her to wake up. But when she did, she was happy to put the news on in her room. That was when I first saw a picture of Saddam and the place where he was caught.

I could never have imagined the way he looked, with his beard and long hair. The Americans were searching him and I wondered if they thought he might be carrying something dangerous.

The idea that the president of my country was hiding in a hole in the ground was equally shocking. When I saw a photo of the hole, it was incredible to me that he could hide there and that the Americans could even find it!

My dad once told me that in 1959 Saddam had hidden in the same area, after trying to help overthrow the government. I wondered if the hole where the Americans found him was the same one he'd used back then. They called it a 'spider hole', but to me, it was more like a 'rat hole'. Saddam was hiding like a rat. I heard that he did not even fight the Americans when they captured him. He just gave up. Was this the man who had been telling us to fight to the death?

As the day went on, I started getting e-mails from my friends at the University of Pennsylvania congratulating me on the news and asking for my opinion about it. I told them all that even though it was an incredible day, the troubles for my country are not over. There will still be fighting between Iraqis and Americans and the problems in Iraq will continue. I know they will be fixed one day, but I am not sure exactly when that will be.

When I e-mailed my dad, he told me not to worry. He reminded me that even though the regime had only ended recently, Saddam had died in the hearts of many Iraqis long ago. The solutions to Iraq's problems will come in time.

I wrote a goodbye to my dad and went back on to the Internet to see more news. It was then that I first saw the press conference when Paul Bremer told the world: 'We got him.' What struck me the most was not what Bremer said, but the reaction of the people in the room. They stood up and cheered.

There were strong reactions in many places in Iraq. My sister Aula told me later that some girls in her school were so happy that they were throwing candy and chocolate around. Others were so sad that they wore black. Aula was one of the happy ones, but she said she was still sad to see our president treated as a prisoner.

A part of me felt sad too, but not because Saddam was gone. I think it was just because we were used to seeing him like a lion. We were used to being afraid. But now, the lion is gone. I hope the fear will go away too.